Every Mask
I Tried On

Every Mask
I Tried On

Stories by

Alina Stefanescu

BRIGHT
HORSE
BOOKS

Brighthorse Books
13202 N River Drive
Omaha, NE 68112
brighthorsebooks.com

ISBN: 978-1-944467-08-1

Cover Photo: Patrick Coryell
Cover Design: Alina Stefanescu
Author Photo: Patrick Coryell

For permission to reproduce selections from this book, contact the editors at info@brighthorsebooks.com. For information about Brighthorse Books and the Brighthorse Prize, visit us on the web at brighthorsebooks.com.

Brighthorse books are distributed to the trade through Ingram Book Group and its distribution partners. For more information, go to https://ipage.ingramcontent.com/ipage/li001.jsp.

For the Old Professor and José
from my devoted, dark little heart

CONTENTS

SLITS FOR HIS EYES

In every mask I tried on, there were slits for his
eyes.... My savior. My witness.
—from *Bend Sinister*
by Vladimir Nabokov

IN THE SEASON
OF THE BEARD

You have no idea how much it costs to get a hardwood floor re-stained, my sister says.

You're right, I laugh. And remind me again why we're still married to American men.

She snorts. Because they look good in stadiums.

We sit together quiet for a second. "I hear the vacuum cleaner roaring from her television screen, warning idle women that we could be doing something busy yet self-defeating." The daily terrorism of worthless tasks which amp the accumulative unappreciations. We're avoiding gluten, martyrdom, and other founts of gloom in our late-thirties.

She sighs.

I sigh.

She sighs back.

Before we return to the houses and the husbands and unstarved children, my sister and I do this thing we call *snartling,* where we laugh through our noses and admire our own snark. Snartle snartle.

Kiss kiss, I say.

Kissie kissie, she says.

"I hang up the phone, absorb highway traffic I can only hear at night when the kids sleep and eighteen-wheelers leave long hollow sounds in the air. The sound of nothing urgent—all the *OM* I need.

Your sister, José affirms.

The man is all beard tonight—all bush, barbed vibes and

pungent whiskey. I reach up to stroke a whisker. A beard in the room is a rock in the fist. An enchantment. The last glimpse of a lighthouse before the mist muddles it.

I'm proud of you, I acknowledge, given that he lost his job at the planetarium two days ago.

For what?

For keeping the beard.

Some men indulge dramatic feats of self-mutilation during the middling era. But not José.

I'm the resident performance artist, he cringes. A lucky man, right?

Possible. You're definitely not a bio computer.

His grunt changes tenor. From irked grunt to absorbed grunt lies a space of less than two inches.

If you've ever tried to comfort a man during a rich menstrual season with half your mouth still numb from molar cavity fillings, you know where this is going. You know this has nowhere to go. You know it is a hot night, heavy with the racket of spring peeper frogs and the odor of wisteria. A pocket of silence between highway traffic reveals itself as a laceration—a wound requiring attention.

José grunts and sands the porch wood. I have nothing to do except offer feedback. That plank looks more even than the other one. Also: I love my sister, but feminism has failed us.

He says the planks are the same. My opinions aren't well-formed. My opinions are influenced by bad lighting.

Do you love me? I wonder.

Of course. What's the point in verbalizing the obvious? It's not going to rain.

I guess that's true.

Maybe love is the wrong word to use since it's usually the expression that comes most freely when you're on your way out a door rushing towards another. If José said I love you, honey and kissed me on his way to work, my knee would ravage his testes in one swift swing.

You can love me later. That's what I told the boyfriend who liked to play house in college. He was a nice, honest engineer, but the math led him to new combinations of emotional needs and demands beyond the realm of my arithmetic feelings. We had four chairs, one table, a decent couch—why muddle the solid physics? If one plus one winds up two, what else need we add to the equation?

One plus one equals two. Good stuff. The limit of my interpersonal calculations.

•

Don't peek—I'm working on a special something.

José's voice is fragile as birthday party balloons. Under his palm, a couple of unlined white notecards with inspirational quotes copied from church billboards.

Driving back from an outdoor movie festival last week, I waited patiently as he pulled into a ditch outside the Presbyterian place to jot down a saying. The same saying he produces on a notecard with hearts tonight.

I have a little surprise for you, he says, waving the notecard.

It's not a surprise, I remind him. I was there.

He shrugs, a wounded preschooler lamenting a crooked rainbow. He says, I thought you'd like it. He says, It's not perfect, but it's the thought that counts. He says, There's no way to surprise you.

The notecard begs to be magnetized while the man plays for sympathy. His sister works as a psychic for the Nebraska Board of Education. Half of José is the kid who grew up playing games with her. Half his games don't exist.

Try harder, I suggest.

Try to remember how it feels to play a game where the other player invents the rules. Think how it feels to keep losing. Times we play for fear of missing the game, losing the player himself.

I can't do it, honey.

José refuses to play racketball—his planetarium co-workers will be there. They're going to feel all this pity for me and then I'll be compelled to comfort them or make them feel better and there will be this ironic moment when I become a cockroach and everyone will feel better because their pity will be legitimate and my comforting noises will be incomprehensible.

The kids love badminton. Hit a birdie with them.

There's a paradox in which you seek a certain outcome by using methods that repudiate the possibility of the outcome. Say, for example, you try to make a relationship work while paying lip service to the belief that it won't.

Fighting for peace is like fucking for chastity: that's how Stephen King phrased this paradox of self-defeating behavior.

My partner hopes to surprise me by consistently engaging in actions I have described as unsurprising. Maybe he's lying to himself. Maybe he doesn't want to surprise me. Maybe he wants to make me feel cheap. Maybe the fruit of our love is made by child workers in China.

And maybe you don't want peace. Cause g-d knows no right mind attached to a living body wants chastity.

So what did your sister want?

José's cheeks are flushed from batting the birdie. He looks defeated but handsome. He looks hot when he's defeated and hotter when he's not worried about it.

Oh, nothing. It takes a village to raise kids these days.

He chuckles then checks my breath for pink wine

product.

It takes a village to tell a man what's wrong with the current intimacy industry.

You want to visit Africa? He sounds surprised, eyebrows ascendant like doves in a Catholic mural, wistful.

I'm chafing beneath the gilded awning of his hope. There is a blur in my head which one might call resentment, but the expression of this would hurt José. A hurt husband is a weapon of mass destruction. A wounded male ego is relentless in its refusal for reconciliation.

I read retaliation in the runes along his forehead.

You're the best husband ever, I offer.

My desire escalates into a steady buzzing. Maybe tinnitus.

He rubs his beard in self-defense.

A vixen wails from inside the woods. I envy her vocalization. But not her *chaleur*—the heat is a daily chest-flutter and a flush. I know the heat by heart.

You only think that since I left the Catholic Church, he says.

You can't leave the Catholic Church—you've been baptized into it, honey. Your name is on a golden scroll somewhere.

You like me because I lapsed.

He is petulant and growing less hot by the minute. But he has a point. Nothing raunchier than a lapsed Catholic—not since Walker Percy became a literary sex symbol and a poster boy for whiskey-sodden existentialism.

And that scar on his forehead that resembles two thorn marks—the residue of a noble moment, a crown of thorns past—very hot?

I'm not saying I'm a sadist. I'm not exposing a secret bias against traditional religions. I'm just saying the beliefs we leave behind are made precious by the fact of our having left them.

I don't like you because you lapsed…but I like the lapsing part of you.

José wanders towards the restroom seeking baby powder. I think about how we've been married for nine years and the lapse resembles a racetrack we keep running around. Taking turns leaves one in the middle waving and watching while the other runs. But we never run into each other. We don't even run into each other when we exchange places.

The pain in my thighs says I'm the runner right now.

José waits and waves from a motionless, inaccessible middle.

I love you, he shouts.

I never wanted to get married so I keep running. Because marriage is one way of running in circles around the things we've done to keep sleeping together.

•

I started to use the word *love* about José after learning he'd been a faithful apostle of the tooth fairy until age eleven. He wasn't just a follower but an apostle, an all-out, nylon-robed evangelist for under-the-pillow magic and pixie dust.

I love you, he shouts.

I started to use the word *feminist* again when I realized my fairy-loving heartthrob could only manage one thought at a time. This tendency was solidified by the passage of three children through my once private, suddenly-public parts.

I started to use the word *weenie-face* again when nurses expressed concern for my husband—it's the dads that pass out during childbirth, you know—as my uterus expelled small mammals from kettle-warm womb.

I started to cry when the kids asked me to read stories that end with *forever*.

And there's José—a good man, by most measures—but prone to depressive events. Evolution abandoned husbands in the cave of their own construing. When a man talks about his garage or workshop, I imagine a car full of empty aluminum Coors. I imagine they must have wanted to make something but then realized it was pointless. Like dusting. I've read sufficient Bertrand Russell to know better than dusting. Let the dust revamp the living room while I post the chronological progression on social media. I want my mother-in-law to like it. If she likes it with a heart, I'll probably hate her for liking something I want her to hate and thinking she can like her way back into this wicked little, anti-gun heart.

Enter the beard José grows when things turn shifty and he isn't sure which man to be anymore. The way a beard disguises the lower face, hides the lines around the mouth, allows it to function as a mask.

If you think a man doesn't need a mask, then you haven't played enough poker. People wearing masks possess an advantage in ordinary life as well as games. Studies show the bigger the mask—or the bushier and broader the beard—the greater its power.

Prize for most disconcerting masks goes to the ones in which a person hides everything except their eyes. Creepiness makes strangers more likely to pay close attention to your words and actions. The mask's advantage comes from concealing my subjectivity while leaving you open. To my interpretation. To whatever I want to discern in your face.

Frankly, I'd rather be objectified than understood. Most days, the stream of Dr. Seuss seeping from my mouth is incomprehensible. I don't want to be taken seriously or treated in an ethical manner—not when my subject remains foreign, not when my nipples have hardened into rubber from nursing his babies, not when feminism has turned into a knitting and gluten-free baking trophy.

I never wanted to be a wife.

I love you, he shouts. The ground sinks as my breath shortens into tiny spurts—I can't run ad infinitum. At some point, José and I will have to change places again. The track spins and spins, a circle inside a circle, my legs stiffen, feet slowing, the sense of motion nearby—José running, my shoes frozen in place, the wave fluttering from my face like a cheap football flag.

I love you, I shout.

I never ever ever wanted to be a wife. But here I am—waving.

What did I want? A fickle, restless, skinny-dipping life. Not one single star but an unpronounceable galaxy. All of it. Every single twinkle.

I love you, I shout.

The envy fills my throat, renders me nauseous, a cartoon wifey, some idiot's sweetheart, waiting for him to notice. It's not his manhood or his penis that I covet—obvious demotions, both.

What I covet is the soft, tangled shrubbery which sprouts across his face, the formidable beard, the homegrown mask. Because the masked person is not a person—not something about which you can tell a true story. Whatever I say will be a story about the mask. Or a story about how fear makes a face look important. And how I listen a little closer to my husband in the season of the beard.

CARPOOL

THERE ARE PARENTS OF East Ridge Middle School students who don't let their children ride the bus. They prefer to wait in the long line of cars coiling onto the main street. I call it the carpool line, but it's really more like a snake.

Anyone who's been in a carpool line knows how the generous ordeal of waiting rounds into a raptor's beak, swallowing ten-minute chunks of time, intervals large enough for puppy flea baths.

Why we are here—these other parents and myself—wasting time with the qualified assurance of possibly creating quality-time opportunities?

Professional women comprise the demographic most likely to avoid the school bus option at all costs. They are also more likely than stay-at-home moms to conduct heated phone conversations at high volumes while waiting.

Conversations about family values reflect a deep resentment and anger in the upper middle classes of America. Blame is easily attached to those stereotypes who happen to be absent from the table during the specific discussion.

It's like I tell the kids: Life is tough, and there's not a single fair hair in it.

•

In the Volkswagen two cars ahead sits Katie Richardson, wife of Dr. Peter Richardson, an eminent cardiologist. Katie went to medical school for six years before quitting. At one point, she says she realized that most people's lives weren't worth saving. Being a doctor didn't follow logically from this premise, so Katie did the next best thing and married a handsome cardiologist whom people called Dr. Peter.

Katie's middle son always waits close to the curb, as if he has better things to do than hang out with his peers. You can tell from the purple lining on his hoodie and the Skittles logo on his baseball cap that he is a Brony. I wonder how Katie copes.

Put-together. That's Katie. She's texting someone on her cell phone, that shiny brown hair loose over her shoulders, fresh from the tennis court showers. I've never known Katie to lose her temper in the carpool line; she's not the honk-and-yell type. Katie prefers her family as an object nestled within the confines of a wooden frame.

Unlike the three screaming boys which race towards her car, stumbling over one another for the front seat, Katie's framed family is something she can hold which cannot hold her back.

•

Marybell Simpson wears her hair cropped close to the skull, a silken red helmet that magnifies the snap of authority in her voice. Being recently divorced, Marybell stays busy serving on multiple committees to beautify and better the city. Her daughter, Carmen, wears black combat boots to school every day and swears she plans to join the French foreign legion as soon as she graduates high school.

When Marybell laughs, you never know what she means by it. Also, you get the sense that the truth will set her free—that it stands behind her assertions of local robberies and vandalism with all the weight of justice. Marybell is the honk-yell-and-curse type.

If I weren't happily married, I'd drive over to Marybell's house with a bottle of Merlot, pull down her pants, and press my tongue deep into her sweeter side. There's something about Marybell that swings either way. What comes off as pressure in the carpool line reveals itself as passion under different circumstances.

•

My husband has only been through the carpool line three times during our eight years of marriage. Women in cars with kids scare me, he claims. A tiny red robin skips over the patio table, bearing witness to his failed endeavor at empathy. Oh, what the birds have seen.

•

Melody Carmichael is the youngest of the six Carmichael kids. They usually wait together, standing in the shape of a kite next to the aloe plants near the front door. People say the Carmichaels are a lovely Christian family. If they added the word precious to this description, one might know what to make of it. Lacking the disingenuousness of precious, however, we are left with something between good people and signposts of the community.

Mrs. Carmichael is the one who drives the van, while her husband, Mr. Carmichael, accompanies her.

Melody wishes her dad would stay home by himself rather than ride with Mom. His contribution to the family ride is unimpressive—he just noodles around the front seat and takes up space, complaining about the air conditioner and any music Mrs. Carmichael seeks to lighten the load.

He's an old man, racing the dimming of memory to get back to his story, the one he has rehearsed and rewritten over family dinners, the one he knows best.

•

Usually, a brown van missing its rear window stops for all the Mexican kids. I admire their extended kinship networks, the way they roll in and out of each other's clothing like family.

It must be nice to be disenfranchised, trapped at the bottom of the social ladder, knowing better than to take an insincere smile for currency.

As the van drives away, I catch the whiff of a song, kids singing and laughing in their secret language. Maybe I'll cook tacos tonight for dinner.

•

Some people believe that all time—the past, the present, and the future—exists simultaneously. I read about it in *Secular Humanist* magazine while getting the oil changed. That's all very fine and good in conjunction with illustrations from the Hubble Space telescope, but things look different when you sit behind the wheel at the East Ridge Middle School carpool line.

If someone paid me to write an article about time for a magazine that can afford fancy illustrations, I would get my head out of the clouds and tell a true story. Maybe explain how time is like citizenship, a participatory delusion, a trick we play with flags and symbols. Looking at 3:55 PM makes it hard to avoid a particular present.

•

As for politics, it's best to adopt a vague stance of acceptance. Agreeing with everyone is easier than you might think. People want you to agree with them more than they want you to be honest or tell the truth about things. So they strike the inconsistencies from the record and offer to refill your drink.

•

Snoopy Hayes has more friends than she knows how to count. Never in my time of PTA luncheons and Boy Scout baking parties have I met a person who didn't just love Snoopy. If someone buries a puppy, Snoopy knows the right Hallmark for the occasion. Being in the carpool line behind Snoopy is like tailgating—the party creeps right along, bumper to bumper, a bevy of giggles.

Her husband, Walter, is a recovering stock broker who found his second calling teaching business classes at the liberal arts college. Whenever we have dinner with Snoopy and Walter, the conversation rolls around to Wall Street. Walter says capitalism runs on the stench of testosterone, the hormone that demands competitive posturing and thrives on unintended conflicts.

Are you talking about the war in Iraq? I asked, trying to sound urbane.

Walter chuckled and Snoopy made a joke about Saddam Hussein being in a foxhole. All of us laughed for lack of anything better to do.

Now, whenever I pass Snoopy in the carpool line, she scrunches down into the driver's seat and pokes her head up, singing—Peekaboo. I'm Saddam Hussein and I'm as dead as a dormouse.

What else can I do but giggle and wave? When it comes to loving life, Snoopy takes the cake.

•

The award for most immaculate carpool line vehicle goes to Lacey Smith and her platinum Lexus. Mr. Smith is her husband. He's also the only man I've ever heard to use the nickname Honey as an expletive.

Maybe that's why Lacey and her two daughters love Sarah Palin—why they call themselves conservatives. Political ideology reminds me of those long, boring pauses that punctuate soap operas and keep people from hearing what the other just said. I try to stay away from politics. To be a conservative is to stick to the story you were telling before your spouse ruined it by having an affair.

•

On our annual trip to the Eastern shore this year, my mother-in-law described time as the distance between heaven and earth. We agreed to disagree on time, the nutritional benefits of Jello, and whether there are special tests administered to verify the Pope's virginity. I just can't imagine how experts could find something approximating a hymen in males.

•

My husband's name is Richard, but after our first baby was born, I started calling him Dick for short. At first, he laughed when I said it, but then he got used to it. We started to feel like I'd always called him Dick, and I'd never been married to a Richard at all.

Phil Danson, our marriage counselor, used to show up in the carpool on Tuesdays when his wife taught water aerobics, but then the Dansons enrolled their kids at Our Lady of the Holy Robe Catholic School and we never see them anymore.

Dick was pissed when he found out about the Danson kids changing schools. They're not even Catholic! he yelled. We stopped using Phil as our marriage counselor after that because Dick said he just couldn't bear giving money to a papist.

Even though I like Phil, I knew better than to argue with Dick about money or marriage counseling or anything related to religion. Dick calls himself a straight-shooting guy and he'll talk your ear off about Masons and Mormons and anyone who doesn't attend our mega-church.

Dick doesn't know that what Phil taught me might have saved our marriage. On our third counseling session, Dick texted to say he was running late, so Phil told me about meeting the Dalai Lama or the Lama's son or some version of the Lama himself.

That's amazing. My voice was serious.

Yes, it was pretty amazing. I'll never forget all the orange...

When Phil got quiet, I figured he was reminiscing. Phil's the kind of man who likes to think about things without making any noise. He folds into himself neat as a plaid pleat.

Look, Meri, I'm not sure I've been fair to you in all this counseling.

Phil, what a funny thing to say. Of course, I'm sure you have. But life doesn't have a fair hair in it, anyway.

The way he laughed, I worried he might come to pieces. I've never seen a man laugh like that before—like he was shaking his fist at an iron, defying the steam to press things flat.

You're an amazing woman, Meri.

I wondered how close Dick might be.

I want you to do something for me. Can you do that? Can you do something for me that will make me feel like a better therapist?

Nodding, I pulled my knees tighter together to flush away the thoughts flooding fast from the unmistakable ache.

Meri, I want you...

Gosh, how I wished he would stop right there.

...to take care of your own needs first.

Is that all, Phil? Say it's not all.

No. There's more. I also want you not to wait for other people to make you happy before you decide to be happy.

Imagine how frivolous and facile it felt to sit and wait for Dick to arrive so we could work on our marriage. Or what we do before one need swells an octave to include another.

Therapists' offices all have the same vinyl smell, the same

boring chairs, the same ambiance of sterility, like nothing good could ever grow there except a cactus.

When Dick showed up, we talked for a little while about boundaries and borders. Then Phil convinced us to start jogging together.

At home, Dick kept pushing back on the borders. I don't understand why we need to talk about borders, he complained.

Maybe so we don't accidentally trespass?

I mean, can you show me the exact borders for our county line? No, no of course you can't! But we still live in this county and name this as our county of residence on tax forms.

He looked agitated. I thought about making veggie lasagna for dinner.

We don't need to know the boundaries to live in this county.... We don't, do we? Do we, honey?

Leaning over to kiss his cheek. 1 was surprised by the way his skin gets softer every year.

No, of course we don't, Dick. We're not mapmakers.

Then Dick told a joke about how the only difference between a redneck and a yuppie is a county line while I washed the zucchini for the lasagna.

•

I don't regret having children. If I had things to do over, I'd probably still waste hours of time renegotiating my place in the daily carpool line.

But I'd like to think I wouldn't stop there. I'd wear more yellow and learn about plants.

Also, I'd admit that time lies in the way we choose to tell it. Maybe consider how the lies wind themselves into our viewpoint. Something about looking in the rearview mirror swipes fiasco from the best everyday face.

MY NAME IS NOT RITA

HE WAS GOING TO write a book about me and it would not be like any other book we'd ever read. It would not be in English. I wasn't English to him but something foreign, a currency to be handled with care. First he would gain knowledge about different interest rates. I could help him with this because it was research. The writing would come later. After months of thorough research laid things bare.

But my name is not Peggy and so I grew less comfortable with the book whose main character was a blonde Peggy, and the brunette was her sad younger sister who had gray eyes.

Why doesn't Peggy have dark hair and gray eyes?

It was a reasonable question.

He said he wanted to spread me out into various characters. You're too much for one woman, he said. That's why you'll find yourself in sisters and female friends.

At the time, I was the announcer for a bluegrass show on the local public radio station. He never listened to the broadcast even when I asked him gently and remembered to say please.

The recording assistant wanted to know how someone could love you without listening to you.

I said we weren't sound waves.

But I also couldn't really answer because there are many ways of listening, and radio is one of them, but there are others that may matter more.

He wrote down what I said in my sleep.

The things he wrote down did not sound like me and so

I asked him not to read them aloud over coffee anymore.

The problem is that he listened to me when I slept but not when I asked him to stop.

It's also love when they agree not to listen, I told the assistant.

She said it sounded like I wasn't sure of myself. On the radio, I came across confident—bluegrass this, bluegrass that—but in the studio I looked tired and less full of life. Maybe I should listen to my radio voice.

I knew it was just a suggestion, but the assistant was nursing a toddler at the time, and the visible impact of suggestions on her personal life was obscene in an unquantifiable way. What was she trying to prove by nursing a mammal with sharp teeth? At what point do we say the trapeze artist is not courageous but actually quite foolish? I waited for someone to get hurt because things are clearer then.

·

After the fireworks display along the river on the fourth of July, he decided to write the book in English. This would give him time to find a translator for the other language, which he had not yet selected. The air was thick with post-firework smoke. He looked at me and said he didn't want to waste a single minute of our precious lives.

When I observed that he had already written much of the book in English, he said that was not important. The decision to write it in English was more important than what he had done before he decided.

The dishwasher broke. I sat on the linoleum floor and cleaned its frothy mouth. But I felt like he put too much emphasis on his decision, and that this emphasis was less a sign of certainty than uncertainty. I could not help feeling there was a weakness in the announcement of a decision. The mayor's decision to fund family values clinics was announced three weeks before rumors of his affair with an intern surfaced.

The dishwasher had to be replaced. In the book, he chastised a female character for purchasing a mid-grade dishwasher. The extra money could have been used in a more artistic fashion.

He denied the connection between my purchase and that of the female he described.

I didn't model that character on you, he said.

But the character had gray eyes.

We broke up when I admitted that, in fact, I did not wish for him to write a book about me. He said this was because I had a career. He said women had become careerists and this was common knowledge.

When I bent forward to kiss him, he said there was nothing left. No reason for us to continue kissing without the book.

Couldn't we just do the stuff we'd be doing in the book? I wondered.

There were moments he left out of the book and these moments had never been written. Some were very happy moments. Like the one when our cheeks ached from laughing.

He said the book was the heart of all the feelings between us. When he explained how pages resembled garden soil, the analogy grew onerous and complex. I could not follow it. I nodded and thought about my assistant. What did she know? Besides, she was nursing.

Later he moved to Maine and published a book dedicated to a girl named Rita. He said she had inspired all of the characters. But the main character's name was Peggy and the only thing different was that, in the book he wrote for Rita, Peggy had gray eyes.

7 STORIES ABOUT GIRL SCARS

1. The Left Eyebrow Suture Marks

Ellen was bewildered—as if the impossible melodrama of reality TV had bungled into her dining room and found a way to pilfer almonds from the pink ceramic tray. Ellen was stunned, the face of which is unbecoming to a perfect wife who kept her figure through three deliveries. She doesn't remember leaving the cabinet door open and the bewilderment deepens when she reaches up to touch the aching eyebrow only to find a smudge of blood that looks like long-ago lipstick.

It wasn't likely her husband would cheat. Unless maybe she hadn't watered him enough. Unless maybe she'd let his soil get dry; an untended man became an angry little boy ready to destroy the castle that wasn't his to enjoy.

Of course there were arguments that sounded like home-game tailgating so she put them out of her mind because what sounded like every living room wasn't abnormal. Ellen adapted to the way in which times had changed, the new trend being one where women watched football with their husbands and yelled asshole in unison. The new did not replace the old. Bean dip recipes were still slipped into purses.

Ellen's husband left a whatnot in the glove compartment, which Ellen found and asked him to explain. He'd gotten very angry—pointed to all her whatnots, including the one on the glass shelves and even some whatnots she'd given away.

Those are antiques, Ellen enunciated carefully. But he was a dentist—he was used to financial liquidity—so she didn't try much harder. How long had she defended the old things only to find herself classed among them? Family heirlooms didn't make sense. Not if you thought about it.

2. The Bolt-Mark Inside the Inner Right Thigh

Isaac interviewed Asylum Candidate #751 for hours. It was impossible to trace her country of origin. He settled for Middle East.

When his son asked why he never felt like throwing the football anymore, Isaac said his work was taxing, which led to a misunderstanding about the nature of his job. I don't take taxes, Isaac explained, I interview political refugees who are seeking asylum.

What's a refugee? his son asked.

A refugee is a woman whose country doesn't exist anymore. A woman who has no place to go.

His son suggested there was space in the guest bedroom.

Asylum Candidate #751 refused to go into detail about her experiences in various refugee camps. He flipped through health documents. When he asked her about the bolt-mark scar inside her inner right thigh, she said, Lebanon was nice.

Did they hurt you? he demanded more aggressively than usual. I can't help you if you don't answer questions, he said.

The men in the refugee camps say that, too. The woman shrugged as if the scene was familiar.

He asked her again and again—How did you get that scar? Where are you from? Where is your family?

The refugee stared straight ahead without saying a word, a talking head whose teleprompter had frozen.

3. The Letter On the Left Hand

She was careful with her allegiances. Determined to be no one but Herself. A girl who sees the world through the prism of *Fleurs du Mal* would not consider wearing the book's T-shirt version. She would not be like Those Churchgoers in their Jesus blazers. The G-d on their shirts was the G-d missing from their hearts and minds.

She fell in love with a linotypist. He tried to teach her about ink and how to operate his letterpress. When she printed her first book, she understood she could say anything. The power of the press was a form of aesthetic liberation.

After things ended with the linotypist, The Girl was left with a glaring indentation on the skin between her thumb and forefinger. Coincidentally, the letter soldered into her skin happened to be the first letter of the linotypist's name. The Girl wore white kid leather gloves to hide the way she had been disenfranchised by his brand.

4. The Four Pock Marks On the Upper Arm

She wore short sleeves but never tank-tops in the summer. She never explained the scars. She was born in Bulgaria and it was none of their business anyway.

5. The Long Thin Scar On the Instep

Walter turned down the Mahler symphony before addressing his son. He also drew in a deep breath and imagined a blonde waving from a double-wide float in the waters of southern Bermuda.

Every time you say *butt* or *dang* or *heck* or words like that, you will have soap in your mouth. Have I made myself clear, Evan?

But Dad! Those aren't curse words!

Those are words expressed in the Spirit of Cursing. It's a slippery slope, Evan. Once you say those words you'll slip into other ones.

Evan stomped into the bathroom as Walter tried to avoid his wife standing arms crossed over her chest in the doorway.

That's fucking absurd and you know it, she hissed.

Walter smiled sarcastically and bid her let him pass, having dishes to do.

I can't enforce that! she said too loudly. His homeschool co-op friends all use words like *dang* and *butt*! What's the big deal?

The big deal is self-control, honeybun. Not using bad language.

He isn't using those words against anyone—just to express frustration.

It's not appropriate. When I was young, we got in trouble for saying fart.

And it made you a better person?

She wanted a fight—Walter could feel it. But he wouldn't participate.

You think being a Puritan works? You think repressing every frustration teaches people not to be frustrated? Where have you seen that, Walter? The reason there are curse words is to set a limit—but you can't outlaw frustration! You can't torture us like that.

The adagio was next. Walter was counting on it.

When Irma cut her foot on the screen door, Walter wondered why his wife always managed to out-think him. They drove to the emergency room with sirens in their heads, Mahler still working his way towards something soft back at the house. The dynamics of his family life came out *forte*. *Forte* til *finale*.

6. *The Horizontal Calf Scar*

At the academic roundtable on recent pop culture trends, the discussion centered on songstress Lana del Rey. Gretel, the only sandy-blonde of the bunch, held her own. The words suggested a possible fourth wave of feminism which the token male on the panel found to be highly implausible. Truly unlikely.

I don't want to like her, Gretel explained to a Sister during coffee hour, but the transgressive part intrigues me. Lana is a new avatar—the sex object gone wrong, the fuckable female who embodies all the maskuline fears about money, rage, moodiness, infidelity, and ulterior motives. I want to extend my research to answer the question of why men enjoy her. Why don't they feel threatened?

The panel is great, Jenny said, resting a hand on Gretel's arm. You are doing a great job of representing us.

Gretel shrugged. One could never be sure.

Men like her because her position is still dependent on their lust. She is only as popular as she can be sexy.

Jenny was right. Melancholy was the New Naughty. Gretel topped off her coffee and reconsidered the full-fat creamer.

You're right, Jenny. They own their automaton-gone-awry. She can never become undesirable and still matter. I'm attracted to the sad, plaintive moan of the noir-ish sexpot who knows her expiration date.

It took twenty-four stitches to suture the stab wound on Gretel's calf. The Lana del Rey acolyte had been arrested after tripping over a wheelchair ramp as he ran towards the parking garage door. He told the police the panel disturbed him—how Gretel represented all that was ugly and awful about female jealousy these days. That girl was just jealous of Lana. Of course there were others whom he found guilty of the same. It bothered him that these women didn't believe in beauty. How could they get through life without holding anything sacred?

7. The Fingernail Scar on the Right Elbow

Vivi wants it to be special, but there aren't many holidays coming up except Halloween and who wants to miss out on the costume parties?

We can go to the parties and then lose our virginity to each other afterwards, Marcus says brightly. His eyes are the color of indian arrowheads. They strike a chord loose in her.

But the parties will end late and then we'll be tired. Vivi sighs. She doesn't want to explain how the first time should be special and unhurried—not the last breaths of a night but the air of the night itself. A whole thing.

That's it! What about the hunter's moon?

Marcus laughs—What about it?

The first full moon in October when the hunters can see all the deer perfectly because the moon lights up the landscape.

She didn't tell Marcus this was perfect because a full moon could only be a whole moon. An unblemished pie, intact. An entire circle.

Whatever you want, baby. I can wait until you're ready. I mean, I can't wait but I can. For you.

On the night of the hunter's moon, they drove out to the oilfields near the county airport. Nodding donkeys moved up and down, up and down, their lazy metal heads offering their assent.

Those donkeys are pretty suggestive, Marcus joked.

Yes, they are, Vivi blushed. But he couldn't see the pink creep across her cheeks because the light didn't reach into the car. Vivi hadn't considered the moon might somehow be limited.

He kissed her and began to unbutton the blouse she had chosen with tiny green buttons intended to increase the excitement of what was to come.

Shouldn't we go outside and lay on the blanket? she asked, surprised to find herself restless, impatient, somehow distracted.

Hmmmmm, I don't know, baby. What if a truck drives by and sees us? I mean, we'll be out in the open, exposed for all the world to see.

Vivi sighed—there were no trees nearby. Only a silver field dotted by derricks and donkeys. It was quiet inside the car. She'd forgotten to bring the special CD they'd made for the occasion. Each had chosen six songs, and Vivi had placed Marcus' songs at the end because she couldn't quite envision making love with Trent Reznor braying in the background.

Maybe we should move to the backseat, Marcus murmured, his lips running along her collarbone. It felt nice, but his breath sounded labored, like the heavy percussion which sometimes ruins a jazz set. Vivi clambered through the space between seats and stretched across the back where her head butted firmly against the door and one knee bent upwards, jammed against the seat cushion. It didn't hurt when he went in, but she could hardly make out his face from the car's sudden shadows. The old Buick rocked back and forth as Vivi's head pressed hard into the door and one arm fell asleep under the weight of Marcus' torso.

There were so many things she hadn't anticipated. Like the old metal ashtrays built into the back doors of the aged sedan. Like the sharpness of metal—and the way everything grows an edge where sex is concerned.

Marcus called the half-moon scar on her elbow a keepsake. But it wasn't an honest keepsake. It wasn't even a full moon. Just some half-etched fingernail moon, worthless and hard to remember.

WHAT I LEARNED ABOUT FEMINISM IN BOSTON

WHILE SHARING A FUTON with this fellow that studied corporate law at Harvard, I read books about 19th century feminists. The vibrant bow-ties worn by campus professors seemed connected to the books. There was also a discreet, unspoken relationship between the books, the bowties, and the numerous cardinals perched in bushes near brick buildings.

In Harvard Square, I purchased a bagel and coffee from a newsstand and read the latest issue of *Z-mag* straight off the rack.

The cardinals watched the pigeons peck round my feet for crumbs.

An outspoken homeless woman leaned against her shopping cart and jabbered quickly to the cardinals. She ordered them around. When she turned towards me, I assumed a cordial expression. The homeless woman said the cardinals were there for a reason. This reason was simple. The presence of cardinals meant someone was trying to contact me from heaven.

I did not intend to get trapped in this conversation since 1) I don't know anyone in heaven 2) I have a long-term fear of being inauthentic when conversing with homeless persons. As a result of the intersection between dread, fear, and bibliophilia, I read whenever I wasn't walking or trying to avoid conversations with strangers.

•

INSIDE MY BACKPACK, 19TH century feminists issued important proclamations. The feminists kept their distance from the male novelists. They wanted nothing to do with The Bostonians.

After walking around Harvard Square for an hour, the battle on my back, I realized it wasn't possible to enjoy Henry James without harming all women. Ever. Throughout human history. Henry had played his hand like a fox, lambasting local feminist progressives while mounting a scathing critique of Boston elite.

I couldn't be a part of Henry's plot. Even if I agreed that Boston fit the bill. Even if Harvard was home to lukewarm liberals who planned expensive, ostentatious events no karma-fearing leftist would frequent.

Hear me out. If you wanted to attend an anti-Iraq war protest, you had to hop the bus to M.I.T. and join the nerd revolt. The only revolution at Harvard involved revolving doors for Larry Summers and various neoliberal lobbyists.

Not to worry, I found shelter beneath M.I.T.'s hardcore left wing. It was warm if slightly robotic and mechanical during marches. I needed a nesty underwing kind of thing just then.

See, the man I was boinking at the time had a secret affinity for John Ruskin. We sat near the river and gulped cheap porto that stained our lips purple.

He tried to make me see that women had a natural, scientific longing for marriage and motherhood. His lovely purple lips quivered when I denied this.

I maintained that women wanted the same things as men. There was a swinger's club down the street, and most of its members were women.

But the man was morose.

Whenever I spoke, a small fluffy cloud of unhappy descended upon his face.

He wished I wasn't so opinionated.

If I wasn't so opinionated, I might learn a thing or two about corporate law.

I might learn how to wash a scrub brush after scraping dishes.

I might learn why we close windows when the weather-dude warns of rain.

The cloud jiggled as the man formulated a question, namely: If women could do whatEVER they wanted, then who would do the marriage and motherhood part?

I knew this was a rhetorical question because he rarely asked questions that weren't already answered.

As he spoke, I saw an anti-home person performing fellatio beneath a bush further down the bank.

I wondered what it felt like to fellate another anti-homer of the same possible sex.

I wondered if pro-home persons hooked up with anti-home persons on the banks of River Charles frequently.

As I wondered, the man worried. He worried about the future of all the world's children but mostly those of our particular mammalian species. Human children were a handful.

We agreed that the children were innocent.

Nevertheless, the man with whom I was bumping uglies saw natural divisions between the sexes where I saw billboards and over-saturated socializations.

We couldn't agree on this. We couldn't even agree to disagree as to whether it was a chicken or an egg. We argued over whether poultry was involved.

•

WHEN I DECLINED TO satisfy his request for light BDSM, the man accused me of spending excess time with transgendered persons. He didn't get why my voice had grown less womanly.

He tried to tie me to the floor heater with a green silk scarf and eventually gave up.

He stood near the window and repeated the word *strident*.

There was a nice group of second-wave feminists at the law school who had kept their womanly charms. The man said I should hang out with them. They might be a good influence.

But I didn't see how I could be influenced if my nature was yearning for motherhood and marriage. He made it sound like femininity was a social construct, a role I might learn to play perfectly, given proper grooming. But I saw a dark hole where the best and brightest should be.

I saw that Harvard Law School 1) a dark abyss and 2) a factory for fallacious arguments.

Also: the man I was banging could not just cry Nature! and then fall back on Nurture!

Especially since Nurture was my position.

Since the man didn't even own a couch. I said the least he ought to grant me included a position.

At which point he insisted that, in fact, Socialization had been my position. And word that begins with *S* designates a different concept than a word which begins with *N*. Connotations cause unplanned alterations. As a result, he maintained that Nurture was still available.

The man I boinked for a year and nearly married was a fool of the first realm.

The man would do well to read a few of those Victorian novels I'd stolen from Harvard Library. It was easier to manage telepathy with cardinals than speak.

P.C.B.

THE CONFERENCE ROOM WAS magnificent, the applause purpled by shameless enthusiasm. His paper had been delivered in a steady, unruffled voice untrammeled by tics. The title, P.C.B. in Secondary Social Networks, implied elegance and veracity. A good title permitted a man to discuss the disinhibited lechery of a latchkey kid with two full hours to burn before the parents returned.

A scientist of reknown, a trendsetter in his field, he studied pre-copulatory behavior, the series of linear and occasionally geometric patterns which both indicate and secure the coming coition. Light verbal banter was the beginning and pivot point.

When consulting with church marriage groups, he recommended self-presentation with open vistas of chest and abdomen. Pure modesty indicated an aversion to sex, but coy modesty was wildly successful. A gauze of grins and batted eyes might easily be taken for giddiness. Middle-aged men needed giddiness—this was why they sought younger women. The wives should consider dabbing napkins over parted lips in a soft-porn sort of way. This was a global hit on the P.C.B. circuit. He was happy to share any further data that might improve their marriage behavior.

Between airports, he watched the social interactions which accumulated in security checks.

To the Lions Club, he urged grooming and gum. Also, an ease of manner which implied the dice was loaded from the start. Romantic but firm. Fatalistic but spontaneous and unexpected as a treasure hunt. The men always laughed when he concluded, X marks the spot.

At the Young Professional Women's Association, he identified the roadblocks posed by second-wave feminism. Though the third wave corrected such errors, an emerging fourth wave threatened to dismantle P.C.B. entirely. He did not tell the professional women how much he despised this fourth wave. Instead, he urged them to aim for disconnected physical gestures which disconcerted and provoked others to think of sex. This was readily accomplished through an approach to food and conversation implying underlying fecundity with the promise of birth control.

For the Baptist Youth Cabal, he emphasized integrity. Anything related to Oldsmobiles was a shoo-in. Did their parents or grandparents have an Oldsmobile they could borrow? A sudden interest in whippoorwills as time-telling devices was clear P.C.B.—clear as dusk.

At night, he laid on the ice cold kitchen tile and reviewed the day's glances—what others had shown him in unmarked cars. The neon lights of minimarts destroyed P.C.B. in every circumstance. This would be the subject of his forthcoming paper, but the title eluded him.

Speaking to the national AARP convention, he admired their tenacity. They were beyond verbiage and nonsense. He said as much. They clapped without inhibition. They radiated P.C.B. He could not imagine screwing an entire room of elderly people in one night. Perhaps he would return.

To the events planner, he acknowledged the limited parameters of a word like *love* in the global scheme of things. A word like *love* amounts, at most, to a moment— this moment—the here and now between us is fraught and frizzy with P.C.B. She administered an unoriginal though enthusiastic blowjob.

MOTHER-IN-LAW
COLLECTION

I'M NO MATA HARI, but I'm good at what it takes to get a mother-in-law. Not good at the marriages or the swindle of supper and spouses, mind you, but a woman's got to be specialized or her duties get outsourced to Japanese massage parlors. What *Consumer Reports* won't tell you is that the Thai massage parlors are the cheapest, but that's because the girls are trafficked and once they get here they can't go back for fear of ruining their husband's honor.

What I like about mothers-in-law is how they're past all that. They treat honor like a rest stop along the early travel routes and they don't do rest stops anymore but head straight for the 24-hour neon gas stations. Honor is legend on a road atlas, but now we have GPS and even the legends are disposable.

In seventh grade, I started collecting postage stamps, the unmarked pristine variety. The kind you have to touch with gloves so none of the backs got sticky. There are actually special lamps used by Philatelists to check the back of a stamp for marking. I didn't have one of these lamps, but I knew about them.

My first mother-in-law bonded with me over the stamp collection. Ginny always wanted George to marry a nice girl, she said, a girl with her head on her shoulders screwed tight. When she saw the shelf in my condo—an entire shelf of stamp albums, each stamp classified by date and value— Ginny clapped her hands together, said the rehearsal dinner should have a philatelic theme.

George and I started a vegetable garden. We killed our first tomato crop by having sex too close in a sensitive phase in the lunar cycle. But the cucumbers grew big as elbows.

My grandfather died. George went to the funeral with me and helped carry the casket. They used the word *bore* to describe men who carry caskets, as in the man bore the casket. He was a true bearer of caskets, that George. But caskets are not crosses, no matter how you phrase it.

In addition to all his power tools, my grandfather left me his Romanian stamp collection—seven albums of stamps minted by Romania's communist government prior to his defection. He brought the stamps with him to America but left behind photos, maybe the ones with the wife and daughter he kept in a bottom drawer. The photos remained uneasy access.

I knew the stamps were worth a fortune, but valuation was out of my league so I started attending the stamp club on Thursday nights at the library. That's where I met Richard, who knew more about stamps than Teddy Kennedy.

George found out about the affair when I left my stamp books in the living room one Thursday night. George bore the stamp albums with the same diligence he'd offered the casket. He brought the albums to the library, but I wasn't there. That's because I was having sex with Richard at the high school ballpark under the aluminum bleachers.

Ginny and George could never trust me again. George didn't say much except he wanted a divorce and he didn't want the house so Richard moved in. After Richard and I got married, we had to share a car for a month while his motorcycle got repaired. When I drove Richard to work at the newspaper in the mornings, sometimes Ginny would be standing alone outside the library holding a white poster board sign that said some mumbo jumbo about stamp clubs being Sodom and how they didn't need to rest at the library.

When I moved, Ginny always moved back. But we didn't talk or wave.

•

Richard's mother was a widow whose husband died young because he was a stock car racer and there weren't any rules to protect racers back then. I loved talking to Sara Beth about history. She didn't care a thing about stamps, but she could name every moonshine still in the state of Georgia because her daddy had been a tripper, one of the secret ghosts that hauled illegal liquor from stills to urban centers in the South.

Sara Beth loved to watch him work on his car inside the old barn.

He drove a 1940 Ford and he painted that car a different color just about every week to avoid gettin' caught by the law. When Sara Beth talked about how fast her daddy drove, she pulled the air through her teeth sharp and fast, like a popper toy or a penny whistle.

I told SaraBeth it sounded like an exciting childhood, and she knew to take it as a compliment—there was that sense of things between us.

When Richard found a job in Opelika, I favored Sara Beth so much it made the move look too much like hazard. I started giving fabric away and drawing X's through calendar pages. Richard worried I was moping around the house and not getting out.

Richard, I'm avoiding the hazards. The deluge of slippery acorns were not easy to avoid in November.

Richard was sympathetic after I read him an article in the doctor's waiting room about how hormones make women angry.

Well, you are pissed a lot. But you didn't seem pissed last night when we were one big naked knot of limbs.

I wasn't pissed then—and I'm not pissed now. But I feel like you're always trying to decipher me, un-code my words like I'm the kind of person who doesn't just say what she means.

He rubbed his beard and said women can be funny that way. They tell you they're sad when they're actually raging. A good man smells the hops before the brew and sets into motion a pre-apocalyptic sex scene between two married humans fully aware that the world might end at any moment. A good man doesn't try to fix a heart with a hammer and duct tape. A good woman gives up her mother-in-law collection.

WOMAN CONFRONTING
THE LONGITUDES
OF HOUSEWORK

Antonio looked comical in reading glasses, which is why I could not take his complaints about housework seriously. Ten years earlier and the scene would be a joke we followed with shots of Wild Turkey, but time is not my strong point; thus I missed the prominent furrow in his brow and the Biblical lines in his cheeks, which hid a yearning for justice.

It's not as if tidiness matters in the grand scheme of things—not what you'll wish you'd done better on your deathbed. A deathbed scene couldn't hurt.

Is that so? he said, construing the unlikely as if it were likely and my angle all wrong.

His need was not to be tampered with, but I had nothing better to do, and so I sat on the divan and lined up his slippers, hoping the arrangement might please him—a wife at his feet and two slippers waiting like soldiers for marching orders.

It wasn't what he wanted, but it had the form of what he wanted with attendant nurturing posture, the eyes open wide in supplication. It was a semblance.

Antonio's book sprawled open in his lap. He was not impressed. If it was montage he wanted, the remote was on the armrest. He could find better poses on commercials in less than three seconds.

Both the fact and the fiction summarily rejected, Antonio glared at me through the dark green rims of his horrid reading glasses, which he wore whenever he sat down to pretend he might read a book. As if he'd ever read a book since we got Netflix. As if the idea of reading glasses could be an event I might digest soberly rather than a costume he diddled me through.

Maybe we should get a maid, I ventured gently as the white gumdrops mingled with the better flavors.

That's fine for you—being a woman of few ideals and principles, but a maid for me would be a nightmare! Whatever you may think, I am not and have never been an elitist—never have I styled myself the sort of chap who pays others to wash his skid marks from underwear.

He could go on and on in this vein for hours if no phone rang to snip it short.

Oh, the phone is ringing in the kitchen. I rose and headed towards the hall.

If it's Richard, please tell him I am too drunk to drive and therefore too soused to go out and visit.

The phone hadn't even whispered. It was quiet and child-like in the receiver. If Antonio was drunk, he had skipped the merry middle-ground and shot straight into the doom-and-gloom Faulkner chapter of inebriation.

I stared at my purse and practiced the French verbs from the cassette. *Essaiez, allez, entrez.* Try, go enter, though *aller* could also be used to invite—*allez avec nous*, or come with us. Coming and going a similar movement in French.

What did Richard say? Antonio bellowed from another room, his voice softened by distance.

Allez, I muttered to myself. There was no call from Richard. The evening was dull as dripping bread, our marriage as vague as a Danilo Kis story, the elements foreshortened into centuries and empires.

From the kitchen of failed quiche to the hallway of discouraging portraits and on towards the hearth of ever-after with Antonio keened on the latter-day love-seat in horrid glasses, that miserable scowl on his face. A misery missing something you could see from across a room but not in the love-seat. Not in the head-of-household where what went wrong.

Should we watch *The Tudors*? I wondered aloud. Thinking life was simplified by small furry pet mammals and creatures which warm the glacial married lap.

Antonio grunted a reluctant assent. He'd seen all the episodes but nevertheless found a smidgen of comfort in soft porn costumed as tribute to period pieces of history. Things grew darker after that cruise to Alaska when Antonio realized he had never set foot in Russia—all those Russians he'd read without once tromping across the soil that grew them. It was a morbid boat ride back, flares of sciatica, disappointed dolphin sightings, the pathos of porpoises and plastic gallon rum.

A rustle in the entryway when suddenly who should appear but my sister-in-law, Esther. Twice married, twice divorced matron of the fine housewifely arts, this Esther.

Hello there, Tony. That husky voice.

Esther, who invited you to interrupt our busy Friday?

With Antonio, one can never tell if he's being honest or sarcastic, since he has stake in neither.

She adjusted her long purple skirt and propped open a bag. I like Esther, really. I appreciate her strong sense of justice and the way she comes across as a hussy—as if she couldn't care less what you think of her gnarled feet in open-toe sandals.

But here's the thing—she has that shameless eye about her, like she could read your palm and then ask for money, like she could see the money in the lines and price accordingly. Not spiritual but realistic. One hand in the pot of ever-after, and that's the only hand she's showing. The only part of her you see. So there wasn't much growing between me and Esther apart from a man.

Story of the world: things growing between females because of a man. Story of the world is not my favorite story, however, and not worth the ink wasted in romance novels.

Esther knits furiously—the clacking needles coinciding with her commentary on daytime television, the decline of quality sushi, the real problem with charter schools and so on. If the needles were silent, Esther would be looking long and slow over them and ambushing us with a poignant stare. Her poignant stares were notable both for their sharp silence and the pointed needles paused mid-air as if to freeze the frame. She had competed in beauty pageants and never won a gold. This part of Esther was apparent in the drama of the poignant stare. Times I wish there had been losing streaks in my adolescence to bequeath dramatic social behaviors which came so easily to Esther.

Whenever Esther visited, the goal was to keep her talking. Antonio listens warily. He watches the needles clatter from the corner of his eye.

I've always said you needed glasses, Tony. Esther harumphs.

These are reading glasses, not distance glasses, he mumbles.

Looks to me like whatever you want to call them will include the word *glasses*. Not even Antonio is fool enough to argue with that.

This is the year when every day feels like the same dreadful morning. The morning of a contest when the winners will be announced but you know you haven't won because the winners are privately told in advance of the public announcement. There is a difference between knowing you haven't won and losing. So today is the day that the losers are announced, and you have ample reason to suspect yourself in their company.

In the den: Esther and Antonio watching television.

In the mirror, my face: the absent, astonished gaze. A woman coming to grips with events.

WHERE I PLACE
MY FINGER

Where I place my eye, I want to place the bullet
Where I place my fascination, I place the pen
Where I place my finger, there is the wound.
As if laying an egg, I place a story.
                    —from *Dark Desires and The Others*
                            by Luisa Valenzuela

CABIN PRESSURE

JOSÉ READ THE STORY on the flight back from Nebraska. The return flight was packed. He was glad there were no layovers.

There was a mother with purple highlights sitting in the row ahead. She had a baby that traveled in a plaid sling close to her body. I heard her tell a person that it was the baby's first flight.

It was a lap baby. The mother made funny noises at the baby and promised to feed it soon, but the baby began to cry.

Passengers conspired against the mother with the crying lap baby. Children were much more obedient in my time, said the woman with glasses who knit through most of the flight. She said the problem was permissive parenting.

The man next to the knitter had restless leg syndrome. He said that being in a cabin with an unhappy baby was the equivalent of waterboarding. Terrorists should be waterboarded to save American lives and freedom, but he was no terrorist.

The knitter clacked her needles.

The baby cried and cried.

I watched José read and tried not to worry about what he was thinking.

A flight attendant in a black nylon skirt asked passengers to remain in their seats for the duration of the flight. She was carrying napkins with logos inked on one corner. The pilot was monitoring cabin pressure. There were technical issues but nothing to worry about.

The mother began nursing the baby. For a few minutes, the baby did not cry.

A balding man with thick eyebrows asked the flight attendant if that mother knew what she was doing. He was recovering from an addiction to pornography, and the sight of possible breast was unpleasant. If he happened to see the breast, it would be harmful. It would threaten his recovery.

The man had a wife and four children at home who depended on him.

He wanted to be a better man.

He could be a better man if it weren't for certain things, including the woman nursing her baby.

The woman should stop nursing in public and find a decent location. The bathroom seemed private enough.

The flight attendant sighed and whispered something carefully to the mother. I couldn't tell what she was saying because her face did not reflect the tenor of the words. A tiny whimpering sound came from the mother. I heard the baby unlatch and then the crying began again.

The knitter sighed and clacked faster.

The balding man leaned back into his chair and shut his eyes like he was beginning a nap.

The flight attendant said no one should stretch their legs or go to the restroom until the pilot cleared the technical issues. All passengers should remain in their seats.

The man with restless leg syndrome said he was a veteran of two foreign wars. The knitter made listening noises. The man said he was a patriot who did not deserve to be waterboarded. What he did in those wars was nothing like terrorism. What he did was so difficult that he had been diagnosed with PTSD afterwards. The crying was like a combat trigger. The crying made him feel like he was in

Guam all over again.

He asked the flight attendant for some whiskey and held up two horizontal fingers.

She said she wasn't sure what drinks were available but she would let him know in a few minutes. Her lipstick was the color of a luau.

José looked up from the paper and said water would be fine. He asked if I could sense a difference in cabin pressure.

I wasn't sure. It could be cabin pressure or lack of sleep. There was no way to tell.

I asked if he had any thoughts on the story.

He smiled and put his head on my shoulder. When his head was on my shoulder, I couldn't see his face without removing his head from my shoulder.

He said it was a good story with an unexpected ending. He enjoyed the surprise at the end, but the story itself lacked a certain force.

The baby hiccuped between wails. The mother made shushing sounds remniscient of movie theatre popcorn machines.

José yawned and said that maybe my verbs weren't muscular enough to carry such a strong story.

OUR FRIEND MIA

MIA PURCHASED THE SMALL peach Vespa because the hue was drum loops and syrup-drizzle glimpsed across a used car lot. What she saw was herself astride the scooter in a black and purple flower rayon skirt floating through silent traffic in an early Italian movie.

I fit into arthouse films, she said.

As her friends, we suspected the medium of poster suited Mia more than the film itself. Mia's mute elegance was hardly plot-driven. And maybe that's where she messed up—in seeing herself as a movie rather than its advertisement, the belief that she was the content itself rather than the promise.

The crossness of our tone is intended to foreshadow problems. All problems begin a petri dish, but the power of magnification blows them into proportions we permit ourselves to take seriously. A virus seems tiny at first but winds up massive. At its best, an epidemic. Though we don't want to scare you because this is not about ebola outbreaks or Jerry Falwell's HIV virus theory. This is about Mia. Our friend Mia.

Her first ride would have been exhilarating if it weren't for things she didn't expect. The two-inch bulb-faced speedometer wobbled and swayed in complete disregard for the frantic flow patterns of rush-hour traffic. Add to this the fact that the skirt did not bloom from between her thighs like a wind-throttled wildflower. Add to this the complete absence of a billowing effect. Accept, instead, the back and forth heaving of a skirt, its motion abrupt as an

Alzheimer's patient scooting his walker over bright linoleum floors in a room with no marked door.

She hid her disappointment inside the unripe tomatoes
procured from a nearby street vendor. Then she parked her
peach dream inside the covered garage and climbed the six
flights of stairs to the apartment. We did not see her climb
the stairs, but we have seen her do it before.

The loft smelled of wet leather and things leftover. Mia
shut the door quietly but did not bolt it (she did not believe
in bolts or helicopter parents), then hung her helmet on
a protruding nail by the door, the one she affectionately
dubbed Hat Rack.

If she owned a small furry mammal, this is the point at
which said creature would swish and bounce against her
ankles, maybe nip at the skin just under her kneecaps. This
would be a Warm Welcome. Instead, she faced the ellipses
of unclumsy silence.

Amir rubbed a palm over his eyes and observed that
she was late. En retard. Again. He did not use French to
express himself the second time. Her Habitual Disinterest
in Others had been facilitated by the choice of a slow-go-
ing Italian scooter. A motorized fascist mobile. What she
needed was a Suzuki motorcycle, or at least a regular bus
route taped inside her eyelids.

Oh, Mia said. How was your day, Amir?

Amir stared at the ficas while speaking, his voice
strained like music from another room where only the bass
was left. No comment on the skirt. No mention of the day
which had just passed, leaving slivers of gold and copper
on the sofa.

We don't remember what he said, but the silence afterward was a spanking.

Mia told us about the scooter and movie. There was a

soundtrack, she whispered, as if music might give her away. A dog barked from the alley behind the building. She knew the dog's name—a small terrier with eyes like a well-nursed baby, eyes that didn't want to stay awake. When Mia spoke, we listened because she couldn't say things she didn't believe, and we were enchanted by the naturalness of her belief in what she said.

We didn't know what to make of Amir. His poetry readings bristled with irrelevant pantomime, the verses worn down by an undercurrent of parody. We like irony up front. We appreciate a good turn of phrase provided it comes out personal. The sympathy we felt for Mia was inexpressible, our pity would result in a further reduction of status. We refused this sympathy. Refused to reduce her to the pitiable face. Certainly it was love for Mia that brought us into an uneasy friendship with Amir.

•

On June 7th, Amir laid in bed. Mia told us he was being tested. For epilepsy. Many Great Writers suffered from epilepsy, and Amir would bear his lot with stoicism. Grit his teeth and suffer the lot of the Greats.

We wanted to check on him—to see if, in fact, Amir looked Great. To verify the suffering itself with extant chapbooks and Marvel comics in hand.

He wore an expression of unenforceable resentment—no object to hold the facial muscles stiff against, no velvet glove to ease the tension—attended by a dirigible accounting sheet of brow furrows and folds. A calculus of x's and o's, the balance sheet unfavorable to any face nearby. Even the grin was bankrupt, the capital of which had been over-solicited. A check marked void before cashing. A half-broken awning still hanging. There was no denying Amir was Magnificent, the suffering edged outward like suburban sprawl. We kept a safe but cordial distance.

Two days later, Mia said the tests had come back negative epilepsy. Amir had been spared the worst, which dramatically magnified the acreage of his suffering.

We brought pot brownies. He suffered in plain sight, pacing from the kitchen to the entryway, pausing to perform his unhappy marriage at us. It was impossible to ignore the Stravinsky involved.

Amir performed it at us even though we had not come to watch, even though the audience converged from accident. We had not expected to share a room with him. The room with the nervous alarm clock flashing red numbers, the unset time a weight one felt obliged to lift—here, let me set the time—the day itself a flat tire one must assemble with engine smoking overhead.

We had not expected Amir to rue his normal health. And Mia? Mia stood near the small potted fern and pretended to examine a frond's underside for perfect brown dots. These are the seeds. A fern with a future bears seeds. No one mentioned fruit. It was clear she wasn't examining the fern while rubbing the same frond rhythmically, patting the frond without drawing any conclusions.

Maybe the future was not about fertility. Maybe Mia wasn't thinking what we thought. For example, she might have been comparing recipes for flan or concocting a related grocery list. Alternately, she might have been concocting an unrelated grocery list. There are many things she might have considered even though the fern was not one of them.

•

It was Jackie who caved. What she'd witnessed in the loft disturbed Jackie so deeply that she purchased a yellow dwarf-rose shrub which she then repotted in sky-blue ceramic container with a braid design along the upper rim.

It's lovely, we assured her, but Jackie was beyond aesthetic succor. You shouldn't go alone, we said. Jackie manages the Avatar & Logo Dept. of a marketing agency. This—and the way she groomed fly away hairs in the hallway mirror—made it clear she preferred to go solo.

I'm going to drop it off after ashtanga, she said. Maybe we can meet for coffee afterwards. Then a grimace in the hallway mirror—high ponytails never stay sleek for long. She would see us later.

•

We forgot to catch the sunset, given the lull of fluoridated lights in respective gyms and the moon who hid her face behind midtown warehouses. Slightly exhausted, we convened at Elmer's place for Irish coffee and coconut scones. I wish Mia was here, Elmer admitted. A few minutes later, he made another wistful Mia pitch while dropping a pinch of flakes into the goldfish bowl. Mia loved feeding my goldfish, he said. She would sit around and feed goldfish all day if it weren't for that narcissist she married.

Jackie blotted her lips with a prefolded paper napkin. She wouldn't go quite as far as Elmer, but she knew for a fact that Mia missed us As Much as we missed her. Especially since Amir's decision to become a rabbi had recast the co-payment of rent from an economic, Marxist-feminist issue to a theological one.

Elmer blanched—A rabbi? When did he say this?

When Jackie stopped by with flowers. After Amir lambasted the insularity of yellow roses. After he expressed scorn for the privilege of household flowers—given all the heedless spiritual suffering in the world, and how did these selfish little flowers help?

Oh, I think your wife could use a little cheer, Jackie had insisted. Doesn't hurt to do good where good is needed.

Elmer asked about Mia—Was she even there?

Mia was there but wordless.

Elmer tilted his head in the classic Greta Garbo. There's no way Mia could continue teaching kindergarten and pay rent on the loft if Amir declined to use his CPA for a second income.

Elmer had a point—we knew he was right—but it seemed beside the point to dwell on what we couldn't alter. Finally, after watching the fish for three vacant, oblong minutes, we asked if Mia liked the flowers.

Of course, Jackie nodded. She loves yellow roses. TS Eliot and shit.

Elmer's eyebrows twitched and hovered over the angora-blue of his eyes. How…he paused and tried again—How…well fuck if I'm not going to come right out and address the elephant in the room—how did Mia look?

Fine. Tired. Like a mayfly on its final descent. Her cheeks were slightly chapped, the overall effect disheveled, as if she was caught between things.

Or maybe between things she'd done and things she needed doing, we mused.

Jackie confirmed it was unclear what Mia was dressing for next. A workplay look about her in an era when we'd gone beyond such idealistic fusions.

We nodded. We'd seen that side of Mia before. The whatnottedness of a loose bun secured with sewing elastic. A half-lit mother's love that failed to keep loneliness from ever coming into her face in late afternoon sunlight. The tawdriness of pale blonde lashes which left the face free of strong topography, a face like Great Plains or some pocket of Nebraska—untouched or over-mined. Hard to say Which Was Which with Mia. Hard to say how ordinary words became tongue twisters when combined.

We concluded that it was the last-peck look. The look-but-don't-touch. The coloring simultaneously not-enough and over much.

•

Amir had never written a poem that surpassed the four-teen-page exegesis of Mia's post-marital abortion. That was four years ago, but murder was still his favorite muse. Mia would do anything for Amir except kill someone. She was pro-choice so the abortion had been a way to placate his anxiety about finances and Montessori preschools. It was a choice she made for him given what he expressed of his Values.

We are pro-choice as well as pro-life. But we think life begins after birth and Kindness To Developing Nations is the single greatest drain on personal karma.

The wife of a rabbi can't ride around on a postal Vespa, Amir declared.

You're not a rabbi yet, Jackie reminded him.

Mia asked if anyone wanted a drink of icy mint water.

We were hydrated and we had to go. We promised to return next week. Amir chanted some litany in Syriac which led us to wonder whether he understood the difference between Hebrew and Aramaic. Elmer posed the question.

Bah, Amir sighed, Syria is not even a country, and Yahweh is a country unto himself.

The days passed like wooden birds striking out from the confines of a Swiss cuckoo clock. There was a time when we could purchase such clocks at Urban Outfitters but not since Mandala Madness had taken over. We felt nostalgia for the cuckoo clocks of earlier purchase. We reminisced about our childhoods through the screen of beloved former toys. We felt united in our hatred of cockroaches. Mostly, though, we missed Our Friend Mia.

We knocked and expressed surprise when Amir opened the door. He was performing hospitality all over the place while Mia rendered charcoal versions of imaginary puppies. It's a new lesson plan, she said.

Amir had grown slimmer—more slender and bony-scaped than Mia—which we suspected to be part of the hold he exercised over her psyche, part and parcel of the guilt he leveraged. I have found my calling, Amir announced obliquely. Elmer looked away. Where was Mia—apart from the sketching—and why was she humming a song we didn't know?

She was laughing without looking at Amir. I've been busy, she said. With work and school and common core. I've been learning how to be a better teacher. The rabbi rolled his eyes and schlepped into the kitchen. Whatever Happened made the well-lit room feel ominous.

We learned that she was trying to sell the Vespa without telling us why.

Why, we said. But it sounded like a question.

The morning sky overcast with heavy strokes of painter's grey could make night believe the day was mad at itself. An almost-angry day. A day where one might take after an Amir and return to one's bed. What was the point of striking out in this weather?

We agreed there were limitations to our vantage point on Mia and Amir. We agreed the weather was a factor in human behavior. But mostly, we missed Our Friend Mia.

DOPPELGÄNGER

Mabel and I played together on weekends. We were like green M&M's—Mabel and Meryl—set apart from the other colors.

The privet shrub was a holy den of lines and untamed columns which Mabel immediately recognized as a temple from the Roman coffee table books. We were girls, well-versed in red tents and undeserving of temples, so the shrub became a secret kept from the neighborhood boys with whom we played video games.

Mabel's dad was a literature professor which explains why he wore bow ties and kept piles of books against the wall of the garage. The books smelled musty; she said he wouldn't miss one or two, and we needed a few books to line the pine straw mattresses in our privet temple.

Sometimes I slipped up and said our private temple, but Mabel pushed her glasses up the bridge of her nose so they settled on the bony speed bump—It's a privet temple, Meryl.

It was Mabel's idea. Everything from the temple to the mattress was Mabel's idea. She read about the mattresses in a book about woodland indians, and the way she told it I was sure she could teach a class on the subject. So we sat in the temple and tore out hundreds of pages and wadded them up in our fists then unwadded only to wad them again until the paper was soft and smooth enough to feel the cotton inside. Soon only the covers were left.

One book was about colonial New England, but the other book was silky, purple, and mysterious. Titled simply

Doppelgängers, I wished we'd read a little before wadding the pages so we could decipher what the title meant.

Mabel played it off by pretending not to care—Doppelgänger? Whatever that means! she snorted. I laughed along but wondered what it meant.

Maybe you could ask your dad, I suggested.

Don't be silly. Then he'd know we stole his book! Do you think my dad is a him-becile? He's a college professor, for G-d's sake.

Him-becile, I muttered under my breath, hoping to add the new word to my Mabel-enhanced vocabulary.

What ruined our temple wasn't the wind because even after it blew the wadded mattress morsels half a mile back into the woods, we probably could have still reclaimed them. It wasn't the professor turning bloodshot red and raging around the backyard about his precious books either. It wasn't even the strawberry-lipgloss kisses Mabel and I exchanged six times as part of a Roman temple ritual. No, it was the boys who ruined our temple—the boys who snuck into the woods behind Mabel's house and found it, the boys who wrote Home of the Dopey Gang for dopey-gangers and dorks!!!! all over the street in pink and white chalk.

I told you so, Mabel remarked with a hand on her bony left hip. Didn't I tell you so, Meryl?

I nodded. She'd warned about the boys and the purple book cover which she thought would be better buried than left as evidence for the professor to find.

I told you boys can't keep secrets or play pretend.

Why? What's wrong with them? I imagined kidneys shaped like pyramids rather than purses.

They're bloody blokes, that's why, she snapped.

I was transfixed by the image of barefoot boys with

bicycle spokes poking out of their skulls and blood pool-
ing in the space below their eyes. Mabel used words like
nobody I've ever known.

Later that summer, we started playing softball on the
church team, but Mabel and I started a base ahead of the
rest. In circles curved like the underside of a giggle, softball
girls talked about nonstop boys.

Mabel said the girls were boy-crazy which meant they
were clueless about the boys' inherent stupidity—and what
boys did to sacred temples or doppelgängers. We practiced
our pitches in the least trafficked corners of the outfield,
my friend Mabel and I, both of us big on knowing but
never telling.

OWLS

THE PORTENTS OF THINGS to come, she promised. Her eyes glistened like two tiny brown slugs inching towards the bridge of her nose.

Ion tried to suppress a shudder. He was too old to shudder. Too auspicious to lament the disgrace of age on a woman's face—the bad landscaping causing sunken pools where there should be smoothness.

He doesn't remember what happened next, but this is how things began. This is what we call a starting point—what happens when we break loose of habit.

Mrs. McClenny is explaining the behavior of the owl to her neighbor. Usually, Ion enjoys talking to Mrs. McClenny because the way she uses words builds in him the steady expectation of a specific location. She speaks about a place in time with the assurance of those generations who lived before places became parking lots.

After her husband died, Mrs. McClenny reached what she called a fork in the road of her life. At this point, she had to choose a future—whether to try and remain the spritely old ballet teacher who chain-smoked outside the church between services, whether to remain faithful to her husband by staying the same. The excuse she gave for changing into a full-time chain smoker who kept up with the neighborhood owls was rheumatoid arthritis. Ion suspected the condition to be a harbinger of latter-day infidelity.

Like most neutral judges, he didn't even know Mrs. McClenny's first name. When he finally asked her, Can I call you something less formal?, she pinched her lips shut like a tortoise and stared straight ahead.

You can call me Athena, she relented.

Is that your first name?

No, she said, pausing to cough, but I'll permit you to call me Athena if you feel the need for an informal reference.

Gradually, Ion began to call her Athena—first in direct conversation, later, in casual remarks to neighbors who laughed perplexedly. People nodded and laughed, acknowledging that there could, in fact, be so many wild animals in the shriveled skin of one old lady.

Athena liked to talk about the barred owl, the one that followed her around the world since she was a knobby-kneed adolescent. The owl that protected me whenever I snuck into the woods to relieve myself, she recalled.

He wonders how she knew the owl was protecting her. He wants to understand its significance. To make sense of it as a signifier.

As the inventor of the so-called signifier as well as the scene, she cannot find words to answer.

•

On Thursday evenings, Ion brings leftover plastic grocery bags and herbal tea to Athena. Usually, they sit in her backyard and drink lukewarm water straight from the kitchen tap. Though she says she likes tea, Athena has never brewed any tea for Ion. Not even the sign of a tea kettle simplifies their habitual interaction.

When the sun slips over the lip of the horizon, towing the day's light behind it, Ion watches Athena shape her mouth into an imitation beak which then emits owl-like sounds and calls. He is impressed by her ability to communicate with winged creatures. He discovers envy can be an attractor.

At first, Ion only wears the vest when working in the garden. The vest is too old and tattered for public display. Every time Ion comes across a feather in the grass, he takes the feather to Athena who stitches it to the vest while describing the bird from which it fell. Soon, Ion's vest resembles a pastiche of broken wings.

The vest feels like home to Ion, which is why he begins to wear it to the grocery store and driver's license office. There is a brief kerfuffle in which Ion invokes a contrived religion to slip past the license photo fashion police. People display their most seasoned company smiles and look for patterns in the linoleum floor tiles.

I'm going to call you Icarus, declares Athena, her tone solemn, baptismal. Ion struggles to hide his delight. When Athena teaches him the basic ballet positions, Icarus finds his feet were meant to open at angles, his gait feels more solid when mimicking a duck.

I don't know how to thank you, Icarus whispers. There is a thank-you in the contour of tears he allows to roll down down his cheeks, a gratitude in what is permitted.

You have nothing to thank me for. You were meant to dance, Icarus. The pirouette looks so natural when you do it.

The sun sets in golden colors, but Icarus perceives the orange as a distinct vibration, a sound wave rising into rubato. He fashions his dance accordingly.

The end is the hardest part. When he tries to find a proper ending point, the curtsey rises as an insult against the bird; an ending dictated by convention does damage to the wings, to the flight of things. The dance is harmless, but the restitution to neighborhood norms—only a fool would attempt it.

Icarus hovers in between. How to choose between eternal flight and the broken bones of landing?

Icarus knows he was not made to land. There are pieces inside him which clamor for flight. The pieces include the loneliness, the fear of failure, the early death of parents, the recent divorce, the way we used others, and the way we define ourselves by how others once used us. The pieces are symptoms, and Icarus is not crazy—he isn't hardwired for this.

The mottled pink sky swallows the feathers—that's one way to think about dusk, sunset, liminal spaces. Icarus says there is something that doesn't match up, and that's what makes it make sense.

He begins with the idea of himself as promulgated by his mother only to find himself paralyzed by a legend, a myth, something to extract beyond the usual story. The memories fail the myth so Icarus flies, hovers mid-air, hopes not to choose.

Athena says his parents failed him—accepted the flesh but not the feathers. Leaning into a pirouette, Icarus thinks she is being too harsh. They didn't fail him (how could failure manage a pirouette) but failed to correct their vision. Failed to see him straight—mistook his skin as an injunction against plumage. Replacing wax with double-stitched seams, Icarus twirls across the yard in his feathered vest, a truly modern man, a resplendent conquistador of sunlight, shadow, and fire. Nothing can melt him back.

LEMON ZINGER CAKE

Two HOURS TO BAKE a lemon zinger cake for my neighbor Anna, who hasn't been the same giddy azalea-lover since her husband left. Two minutes to walk across the street and ring the doorbell. One minute to wait before leaving the cake on the front door stop with a brief note. Eight minutes until a blue pick-up truck pulls into Anna's driveway, and I notice the cake is still there. A smatter of seconds to hope the cake isn't getting over-heated. Eleven minutes before the truck screeches down the street leaving the front door to the house cracked open. Six minutes to debate whether I should re-cross the street and shut the open door. Four minutes hovering near her mailbox wondering whether I should close the door or enter. Five minutes wandering through the house calling Anna, Anna until I reached the master bedroom. One minute to confirm the bloody mess in the shower is the outline of my friend, Anna. Two minutes of high-pitched screams and such. Three minutes to accept the physical evidence of her death. Six minutes to call 911 and establish an assistance procedure for this specific event. Two minutes to wobble out of the house and commence the walk home before remembering the lemon zinger cake. One incommensurable instant to realize the cake is still sitting on the step, its perfect circular form ruined by the imprint of a man's boot in the center. One minute to follow the lemon zinger footprints back to the place where the truck had parked. One minute to replay an image in my head of a man in dark boots running and jumping. Years to accept how the cake

I baked to comfort Anna becomes the district's attorney's key piece of evidence against my friend's murderer. Years to purchase ingredients. Years to bake a lemon zinger cake again. Years, I tell you, missing.

IT'S JUST CHARLES

THERE ARE NEIGHBORS AND there are neighbors, and there are husbands who can't tell the difference.

I'm not going to argue with her, Charles. Seems to me a woman who got her PhD in social engineering knows more than myself about how to organize a neighborhood party.

That tiny little tapping you hear is the sound of a woman putting her foot down several times, each more insistent than the last. This is a conversation I'd rather not have involving the new neighbors.

Charles stares at his omelette. Charles is forever staring at a food item on his plate with his salad fork frozen mid-air. There are days when I can barely handle it. Days when I know our life has become the first take of a frozen broccoli commercial.

Things were fine until Janet turned three and learned the words for all the things she wanted. Dora the Explorer house slippers, rainbow magic wand with glow-in-the-dark stars, ribbons with hot pink initials, a Disney dress, a princess crown, a princess pony with a matching plastic stable, a princess pillow to put on the bed. Things were fine until the socialite neighbors moved in with a little red-haired girl of four. Things were fine until Charles met them and almost blew out his post-vasectomy codpiece.

This is our delightful daughter. Her name is Charlene.

The neighbor spoke in that super-sweet voice men love because it makes them feel bigger. The littler the man, the more he loves the sweet little baby voice these women use.

Charles' mouth hung open like a trailer-park mailbox. He delivered a hoarse hello.

As for me, I hate the name Charlene. Why, what a lovely name, I told the neighbor.

Originally, Charles wanted to name Janet Charlene, but I did not fancy that name at all. I did not fancy naming a girl after a boy especially when the name came out with banjos.

It's been ranked in the top three ugliest girl names for eight years in a row by *Good Housekeeping*, I warned him.

Oh. Charles sighed, his face fell like sitcom birthday cakes. Janet it will be then.

We took photographs of each tooth as it crowned. This was easier than one would think because Janet spent much of that first year crying. She was born with a strong sense of justice.

A month ago, I had that nightmare in which I was wearing my pregnant mumu. The nightmare suggested I could get pregnant. I woke up sweating. Never again. Janet was the best baby in the world.

It would be cruel to have another one, I told Charles, because I could only love the new baby less.

Charles agreed to have his sperm-shooter rerouted. The procedure took less than ninety-eight minutes. Less time than traffic court. I served him fresh chicken noodle soup for an entire week even though there was only one stitch on his scrotum. After Janet's birth, my vagina had more threads per square inch of labia than Charles had on his entire post-surgical scrotum!

Dr. Harding could have at least given you two stitches to make it worth his trouble, I said.

Charles was also astonished by the medical system's inefficiencies. He needed more pain medicine. They had given him enough codeine for a week, but the pain vaulted well past the fourteen-day marker.

I patted Charles on the head. Seems silly to waste that fancy dissolving thread on one single stitch. I'm sure it's not cheap.

Charles nodded. He votes Republican. We see eye-to-eye on fiscal matters.

•

I can't tell you how thrilled I am to know you have a little girl, the neighbor bubbles. Oh I do so hope she and Charlene can be bosom friends....

Of course, I nod.

On our dining room wall hangs a painting of carrier pigeons which guests always remark upon. I think about the painting with its pigeons as the neighbor babbles upwards into play-dates and rented inflatables.

What's your daughter's name? the neighbor finally asks.

Her name is Janet Elizabeth Taylor, I said firmly. Of course I am proud. With a name like that, a girl can do anything.

Janet? the neighbor smiles nervously, her eyes skittling towards the sidewalk cracks. Janet is a very nice name. My mother's name was Janet.

I'm not sure whether the appropriate response would be to say thank you for the compliment or I'm sorry because her mother sounds dead. Avoiding the impasse, I ask whether they considered naming Charlene Janet as a namesake. For her mother.

The neighbor blushes, slightly flustered—Oh yes, we did. Of course we did. My mother was a Kappa Alpha Sigmoid, an incredible woman. But—

My smile is a wide-open begonia blossom.

Well, she lowers her voice to a whisper, I had my heart

set on Janet until my husband pointed out that Janet has been ranked among the top three ugliest girl names for seven years straight by *Good Housekeeping*…

If I didn't feel so sorry for her, I might trample her glossy salmon-colored toenail.

That is a lie, I hiss louder than intended.

The neighbor steps back, her eyebrows quivering with social concern.

Your husband lied to you. And I know this for a fact because I have received *Good Housekeeping* for eight consecutive years, and not once have they published a baby name ranking for ugliest girl names. Not once. Oh, don't think I didn't go looking for such a ranking because really what mother wants to name her child something ugly, but all the looking in the world doesn't make it true. So you can tell your husband it was wrong for him to lie to you and deprive your mother of a namesake just because he liked the name 'Charlene' more than the name 'Janet.' You can tell him I've seen the name 'Charlene' in more dirty magazines than I care to count.

The neighbor clutches the hem of her tennis skirt nervously.

I tell her husbands can be babies, but I hope we can still be friends.

ME AND BIRDIE

June 5

Dean brought me a birdie today.

I thought you might like it, seeing as how you have a nice badminton racquet and all.

I thanked him from the bottom tundra of my heart.

That's a real nice racquet you got there, Dean said, shifting, as if the thought moved from one side of his brain to the other, his happy corpus collosum.

I thanked him from the hippo-most layer of my spirit for having noticed.

Then Dean's wife, Topsy, waved from the car and told Dean yabba yabba late dabba party doo.

I need to go now, said Dean.

I thanked him from the tinder-bough strata of my solar sphere for dropping by.

June 15

I stared at the birdie for twenty-three minutes this morning before finally agreeing to give it a bath.

Afterward, I laid the birdie on a yellow hand towel near the fireplace to keep it from catching cold.

June 16

The birdie proved its loyalty to me and perhaps to Dean by not melting, though if I were in Dean's shoes I'd demand more direct evidence before drawing any long-term conclusions.

I've never looked at Dean's shoes before, but his car is spotless, impeccable, like the fresh face of an ice sculpture at Sunday brunch.

I considered putting birdie in my coat pocket and bringing her to Sunday brunch at the club to see the city's finest careen and covet, taking their agonies out on fruit salad. Being picky about which slice of proscuitto they find on their melon thereby revealing the profusion of their passive-aggressive inclinations.

June 30

Birdie has become very dear to me. Physical proximity and its ensuing familiarity lead me to feel I know things about her hidden from the rest of the world including the universe.

When she stands under the glass lamp, her beautiful red head summoning the sky, I find myself ravaged by the splendid circumference of her white netted gown as if she might for all eternity embalm a sunset.

July 3

I am certain that Birdie spoke to me today, her voice so hushed it was as if a sparrow's underwing fluttered against my ear.

From her words—that is, a string of numbers impeccably launched as a stream sylph-like and sweet as a soliloquy—I feel that she wants to draw closer.

Tonight, I plan to bathe with her in the claw-footed tub. My instinct tells me Birdie will be a bubble to behold. I have reason to believe she will float.

July 14

It is Bastille Day.

More importantly, it is the day I finally assembled the meaning of Birdie's words. The stream of numbers issued by her divine rosy lips were a fibonacci sequence possibly intended to counter the law of plastics.

It broke my heart to discover Birdie has suicidal impulses—that she might provide me with the secret code to her own undoing.

Plastic and rubber are too meagre for Birdie. I can't bear the subtle carbon she holds within.

July 22

It might be Bastille Day. Topsy rolled down her window while I procured my daily mail and yelled something loud and rancid. I have never heard her say anything that wasn't rancid. However, she seemed to be wishing me a happy Bastille Day.

No one in my family is French.

Dean invited himself over to play badminton this weekend.

I convulsed within every fluid ounce of my spleen. Told him it sounded amazing—almost impossible—his proposition seeing as how it might be unpatriotic to play a senseless lawn game so close to Bastille Day and all.

Dean chuckled, called me a funny old crow.

There is nothing more demeaning than wishing one's self suddenly dead.

July 25

I could not believe it when Dean strolled up my driveway

this morning with a badminton racket in his hand.

Let's bat a few birds back and forth, he said.

I refused with all the atomic power of a particle accelerator located within a nuclear submarine factory.

Oh come on. Where's the birdie I gave you? Isn't that a birdie in your pocket?

Dean's irrepressible cruelty is matched only by that of his filthy wife. I tried to explain that Birdie was not a badminton birdie anymore—that she had developed into an exquisite hostess, a poetess of small vowels, a force to be honored and nurtured—but Dean noticed Mr. Schutlz's teenage daughter, Harriet, crossing the street in her softball shorts. Quickly, Dean excused himself, saying he had other plans.

As he scurried down the sidewalk, I removed Birdie from my pocket and whispered sweet soothing nothings into her audubon skin. When Dean turned back around to yell something rancid at me, it's as if the entire street shriveled up, leaving only Birdie and me.

Me and Birdie in the Saturday's sunlight. Birdie and me profiled in the Saturday's early shadows. Love is what's left when you surrender the racket.

TOKETWAT

Even with seven houses between on the neighborhood street, the scent of Meryl still drove me crazy. Three houses away was not far enough to insulate me from her whiff—a crisp, nagging odor, clove cigarettes mingled with breast milk, the color of a faint, faraway rage.

We usually sat in the den of her two-bedroom house with the curtains closed. The faux wood walls stayed bare except for a few family photos. Our occupation consisted of nursing our babies and laughing. In early spring, we scanned digital sewing patterns, and stitched house dresses up-cycled from garish estate-sale curtains.

As mothers, we grew accustomed to certain patterns in sleep cycles, close-out sales, and diaper rashes. We grew in tandem through textbook crises and into their solutions.

•

It helps to have a friend I can trust nearby every time the world ends, I joked to Meryl during a morning walk in that month or two when we decided to consider running a marathon. Too bad that every marathon these days involves promoting some product, and every runner finds themselves plastered in Spandex, racing towards some commercial end or another. Ultimately, it was an unremitting attention to the fine print of things that kept us from running marathons or hawking Avon cosmetics to the lonely widows at Serene Valley Hills. We didn't stay home with the kids to sell shit.

Many things began with ice-cold coffees and our sewing machines. Both of us got into sewing around the same time, though Meryl was much better with patterns and measurements.

I'll never forget her first gift to me: a postpartum maxi-pad sewn from organic silk cloth. It felt like a kiss between my legs.

Meryl, you're terrific…and rather naughty.

Oh come on, Angie! Our privates have been through so much—what, between the men and the birthing of babies—I figured they could use a little pampering…

And so it was that Meryl came to mind every time the monthly cramps raised their glaring red flags across my panties. My partner, Ralph, was horrified to discover that blood stains do not disappear from white organic silk even in the most rigorous wash cycle.

Ralph is actually my husband, but I call him my part-ner to make sure none of my career-driven female friends mistake our relationship for something traditional and repressive. As a stay-at-home-feminist (SAHF), I'm a proud member of the only demographic consistently under-represented by market study research. This is mostly because the SAHF's anti-consumerist ethos keeps us from cutting coupons and joining those online mommy-boards where market research is conducted.

Ralph's sentiments on the subject don't make a smid-gen of difference. Nothing makes a difference in the way I quiver with excitement at seeing the bleedings of bygone months on the soft silk pads as I press them into my underpants.

It's very modern, I told Meryl, as we sat on the back stoop watching the kids tie rope ladders. She wondered whether she should dye the silk fabric to hide the blood stains.

I don't think you should dye it at all. I like the rawness of it. Raw and modern, that's what it is. Straight from the pages of a MOMA gift store catalogue....

The laugh came up like water bubbles in a tub. Oh yeah? I was aiming more for plain old tie-dye.

You could definitely sell some of these pads at Bonnaroo.

I'd gone and put a point on the map. What had I done, she laughed, but gone and launched us into a season of sewing and stitching which ended only with two duffel bags, a sack of stitched Momma pads, and a long bus ride minus husbands and children. Meryl made a T-shirt that said Bonnaroo or Bust that looked really nice laid out over her massive, double-D breasts. We had the time of our lives.

•

Truth be told, we never actually made it to the music festival itself—our bus got a flat tire at a campground in northern Alabama. Still, the campground introduced us to snake-handling and seances, which did wonders for our historical consciousness, particularly the seance in which a Confederate soldier would only communicate through kazoo notes translated into Morse Code.

•

When she wound up with her second bout of mastitis, Meryl knew how to nurse through the pain. We shared the rickety office chair in front of her husband's gigantic computer screen and nursed our babies in tandem. There was so much to do just for the hell of it.

Hey, let's try to find my old friend, Virgil, I suggested, after the French lesbian soft porn lost its luster.

I don't feel like moving. Meryl pouted as she massaged her left breast.

But we didn't have to move—we could sit right here and wander through a whole new world. At the time, down-loading hadn't been established as a form of movement—it straddled the gap between an action and a reaction.

No movement needed, I explained. All we need to do is download World of Warcraft. I cleared my throat and added, Virgil got lost in WoW.

What's WoW?

It didn't take long to explain that World of Warcraft was a massively multiplayer online role-playing game (MMORPG) created in 2004, the favorite online game of freaks and geeks of every combination.

Isn't Virgil the friend from college? The one that became a philosopher? Meryl asked.

He's a philosopher. But a fantasy fan, first and foremost.

Graduate school taught me that if you want to know something about a person's worldview, don't bother to inquire into favorite philosophers—your best bet is to probe their preferred utopias and fantasy worlds. That's where you find ghosts and resilient mental saplings.

The absence of wince led me to assume Meryl was game for online adventure.

First, we have to create a character. I patted Celeste on the back lightly, trying to decide whether to full-out burp her or let her dawdle to sleep on my breast.

•

Goody, goody, Meryl's blue eyes twinkled like swizzle sticks, all trick-or-treat mischief. You know that moment when you share a thought with a person, and you know you've shared it, but neither of you has spelled it out yet? Well, we had one of those moments just before dissolving in giggles.

Both babies asleep, dribbling spittle onto our well-formed cleavages, we rocked back and forth in the black office chairs and selected the busiest, most buxom and scantily-clad female avatar. Meryl wanted to name our avatar Spinoza, but the name was already taken.

Too modern, I mused, though I'm sure all the ancient philosophers are taken as well.

We blew a little time debating whether Plotinus had gone before Israel, and refilled our coffee mugs. After laying Celeste and Mack down on Meryl's bed and carefully ensconcing them inside a fence of pillows, we wandered back into the computer room.

Nursing limited the sorts of prescription pain relief Meryl could use for her mastitis, so she added a dash of whiskey to her coffee.

What's the most ridiculous name we can get away with? she asked, leaning into her laugh. How I love the way she laughs. How it sends chills up my spine and brings bouquets of words to my lips, all florid and bloom-like. Meryl hates flowers, but I'll be damned if sitting near her doesn't feel like being in a tropical greenhouse.

Toketwat, I said, poker-face intact.

Well, I'm sure that won't be taken.

We cackled like a toddler string ensemble. Then she paused to press her lips together, murmuring, Toke-twat… Toke-twat. Tell me if I'm reading you right—to toke is a crime, to have a twat is a liability—therefore, Toketwat, our avatar, a walking criminal liability.

You like it. The words stood solid as curdled milk.

I love it.

So Toketwat was born.

•

Meryl and I whittled away hours of leg-waxing time engrossed in the pixellated world we created for Toketwat. When the husbands complained about frozen pizza for the second night in a row, we laughed conspiratorially, then imagined what they might say if they knew we had killed three different men in our virtual world. There were so many weapons—and so many florid words to describe them. It wasn't a World of Warcraft so much as it was a World of Our Own Crafting.

The parameters of the game kept others from bursting our bubble through physical or emotional contact. Meryl was Meryl, Angie was Angie—intact as two uncircumcised penises—together we were Toketwat. Crimes existed only as violations of unwritten conventions,, and there were no courts to resolve these vague violations. Justice was administered individually or through the collective action of guilds.

We didn't find Virgil. But we found so many other creatures, and we learned how to tell our friends from NPC's, or non-player characters. Like high school mall rats, the NPC's persist in reenacting the same dull repetitions—standing near a building or a bridge, moving right and left, programmed by techies to live their fake lives in behavior loops.

Meryl called me at one AM one night to tell me she knew what she likes so much about Toketwat. She said Toketwat was free from the legacy of unwashed dishes and failed parenting strategies. She's untainted, sighed Meryl.

I guess you're right.

Toketwat started out as a combination of distasteful words. But the conjoining of these words created a new word—a name so distinct and extraordinary that it lacked any precedent. Toketwat: the unblemished word, the unhistoried name. Meryl and me: the gods who made her.

Since Toketwat was our avatar, Meryl and I could not escape being her creators. Our job was to keep her alive. The commitment of creation coincided with the illusion of becoming real through practices and specified rituals. Like

Civil War reenactments, the creators become the players, and the boundary lines are so permeable that creators no longer distinguish between what they're doing and what they're playing.

We played as if the world would end—played as if life depended on it. Hard to explain to an earthling the precise point at which pixel becomes a god thing. Part of the shit a god must do or die.

•

When the kids got the flu, I missed out playing with Meryl for an entire week. By the time everyone felt better, Meryl had joined a guild. Actually, she'd made Toketwat join a guild and earned a battle-hardened thrash blade to boot.

That's awesome, I said, feeling a little disappointed that she'd accomplished so much without me in the wing-span of a single week.

A week turned things around to the point that Meryl didn't even laugh when I brought up her neighbor, a down-right vulgar reductive materialist whose born-again virgin ruse and labia-plastered face represented the summa of sub-urbanoid decadence. She's on her third vagina, I quipped.

Meryl kept typing and clicking, moving Toketwat back and forth across the screen.

Toketwat has a lot of friends now, she said. Her voice lacked its usual vigor.

She's been keeping you busy, eh?

Meryl nodded perfunctorily.

I tried again. If I didn't know any better, I'd say you've become your avatar's social manager.

No laugh. Meryl's laughs were laid up in lounge chairs. Anywhere but here.

It dawned on me that Meryl didn't distinguish between

herself and Toketwat much. When I'd given her a chance to dissociate, she pretended not to hear me.

Well, I just dropped by to say hey and check on things.... The words were spilling from my mouth like jelly beans, or men's group testimonials, a deluge of jelly bean babbles hoping for something to stop the flow before things got stale and then sticky.

Meryl barely nodded. I must have looked as pathetic as I felt walking through the house towards the front door, tripping over a plastic zippy cup in the hallway. If Toketwat was more than pixel dust, I'd have strangled her.

Bye, Meryl, I shouted from the door, trying not to look backwards.

Through the din of the kids' Barney show, I heard her reply, Meryl's not here, but she'll be back in six months or so.

We never talk about it, but that's pretty much what happened.

THE CHANCE OF
THAT HAPPENING

I. *Almost Over*

This night is 82 percent over, eight breaths from finished. My estimate is generous, given gnarled, lumped futon. Coitus looks like spine-injuring work—and I came to play.

Nelson is his name. Air seeps from our awkward lurches, the movement forwards, the bellow of lust billowing towards sleep. This is a soil which promises nothing, a story of low tire pressure.

On his coffee table lies a book about agrimonies.

It allows me to predict future events by observing the weather, he says.

His hands are too large for his shoulders. I like that in a body.

Can you predict what will happen now? My eyes flit towards the futon.

He licks his lips. All the wrong men will continue to gain political power, which is based on obedience. There can't be a dictator if nobody listens to him. There can't be a patriarch we aren't taking seriously.

This Nelson is clearly a feminist. We downshift into mutual respect, our expressions elastic with politeness. I figure the odds of sex just sank.

Outside the window a stagnant bird bath, its water absent the ripple of nipples. A birdhouse with an angular copper roof birds perch atop. No birds inside the house or the bath. No bird swinging. A genuine laerum of significance.

Are we going to mess around? At this point, I'm just curious.

Of course. His voice is gentle. But the chance of that happening is unrelated to actual events.

II. *All At Once*

Things happened all at once with Nelson. Like in the magazine articles. We shared a quizzical silence over the humorous part of a beer commercial. Saw a shooting star in the same Target parking lot. Fought with our respective families over the same Thanksgiving rituals. Took up badminton together and tried to solicit strangers for doubles games. Felt courageous and crazy and slightly superior to other couples, particularly those who didn't play badminton. Made Google maps for daydreamed road-trips and shared new locations via email at work. Cooked linguini from scratch together. Watered tulips together. Cried together. Came together. We called it the all-at-once effect.

All at once we were together like cumulonimbus clouds with no chance of not throwing lightning. But other things happened more slowly. Other events in our lives were drawn out like Herman Hesse novels which took eons to achieve a simple horrific effect.

Take my sister's violation, for example.

After my sister was raped in a public library restroom, the female body grew more onerous and exciting—the perpetual anxiety, the obligatory male escort for badly-lit public areas, the worrying and constant reassessment of risk.

Nelson accompanied me to the trial. My sister looked

pale and thin. On her forehead, the slickened longing of a cat's unfed meow. She had not bleached her roots, which added an element of rural decay to her demeanor. I had misgivings about possible justice.

Initially, the defendant's attorney argued that it wasn't rape because it happened during daylight hours at a library known for its excellent children's programs. Then he argued that the defendant was sure my sister had been trying to seduce him—why else would a girl be hanging out in the nonfiction section near books about stock-car racing? Then he argued that my sister wasn't exactly a virgin so it wasn't the same. Then he argued that rape was a natural, G-d-given biological urge for males, and the defendant could not be faulted for how G-d made him. Then he argued that rape was a social construct. Then he argued that the defendant was a victim who had been molested by an uncle as a child. Then he argued that the defendant was legally crazy. Finally, the defendant's attorney pled no fault on the basis of media programming which encouraged young men to confuse good sex with rape.

My sister sobbed throughout her testimony. The lawyer's arguments included supple ergot.

I felt torn between the need to tell her I loved her and the need to inform her that she looked terrible. How long had it been since she'd had a decent facial? What was her attorney doing to earn that six-figure salary?

Nelson printed out a newspaper picture of the defendant's face and pinned it on the wall near the microwave. Whenever he passed it, Nelson stabbed the picture with his fork, leaving four-holed lines.

The defendant is full of shit, he said.

But the poking made the defendant look holy. Beneath the dust ruffle of dots, the defendant's face acquired a sad, pieta-like expression. By maintaining his victimhood in the face of rape evidence, the defendant had rendered raping holy and sacrosanct. He attracted a fan following of Men's Right's advocates and Sex Addict Recovery groups. He gained a cult following among certain prison populations. My sister didn't keep up with any of this. She moved to a small town in southern France.

When the trial started, Nelson had asked me what I thought the chance might be of my sister moving to Japan to put distance between herself and traumatic memories.

Zero, I'd replied. Zilch.

And I was right. But only because Nelson hadn't mentioned France. Avignon was the last thing on our minds at the time.

III. Sixteen Months Later

The chances remain monogamous. Nelson and I have been dating for sixteen months when I run into a famous writer at a café. Sitting alone at the table near a window, The famous fiction writer, probably writing a good novel. The envy feels fresh and highly-motivated. It gives me courage to approach him.

Did you know I have a thing for empty stairwells? I ask the writer.

He tries to pretend I'm not real, but when I say the same thing again, he relents and looks up from his laptop sternly.

You can find all kinds of detritus there—soiled tissues, eyeglass lenses... I continue. It sounds like the sort of ambiguous thing a writer might like to ponder.

I suppose that's why I write, he mumbles, the torn words broken in the lane.

My thoughts are closer to fear and thrall than sorrow.

I notice goosebumps, the possibility. Words soaked at random by gun-bearing toddlers.

There will always be orderlies in the fields at night and fear on someone's face and the unalterable sadness of loving enemies near and far, Ron says quietly.

What are the odds? I wonder. The famous fiction writer in a cafe quoting himself.

IV. The Odds Are Bad for Women

The badminton net sags in the condominium yard. I spy a birdie less than twenty feet away, nestled between tomato plants in the half-tended, overgrown community garden.

When we moved into the condo, the garden was a big deal. People got together and shared garden tools, talked about college football teams and recent recruitments. Now the unharvested squash has swollen to watermelon-size and no one wants to touch it.

Maybe next year, Rhonda, the green thumb environmental enthusiast, says. Maybe next year when her mother isn't dying.

I tell Nelson about meeting Ron. How slight the odds. The chance being nothing.

That's pretty cool, he says, ruffling my hair. But the odds are tainted by self-reporting bias.

How so?

While more than 18 percent of men say they've had a threesome, only 8 percent of women confess to the same. This leaves a small percentage of females responsible for a vast quality of threesomes.

As usual, Nelson comes across the more diligent feminist.

The odds are rough on women. A majority, or 1 in 1.6, of married women will not masturbate in a year. Odds that a female in her thirties has genital herpes is 1 in 3.

Nelson reports these statistics sorrowfully, and I feel the old urges return—the hunger to know the odds, the chances our promises will wind up broken. In anniversary photos at scenic locations, I glimpse his heroism, the artifice of an epigraph above us.

But I didn't imagine dragging the futon into the dumpster. The odds were never clear on us buying a bed. It's the odds you don't calculate that feel impressive.

V. Hot Times on The Trailhead

I can't guess-timate time from a sun hidden behind trees, but the scent is distinctly juniper, the tunnels of cool air reminiscent of hotel stairwells. Nelson asks what I'm thinking, but it's too sparse to describe.

Thinking if there is a bridge, we should race across it.

Why didn't you become a zoologist if you love animals so much?

Nelson isn't sure. For the same reason I didn't become a veterinarian. I can love animals as a hobby.

I think you are a zoologist at heart. I think you love animals in a way that makes it hard to be a member of one species and live as a human.

My hair smells like a piano recital.

Are you worried about something? he asks encouragingly.

Rather than disappoint him, I nod—because I'm always worried about one thing or another.

He tucks his hand under his belt strap and grins. There is a 2 percent chance something horrendous will happen to us on this hiking trip, Natalie. Not including minor cuts, injuries, hunger, thirst, insomnia, or feelings of unspecified discomfort. It comes as a relief to hear him say this explicitly, even though I don't believe in statistics or the output of any science that presumes itself social. Nelson's confidence deserves a slight prod.

What about a tick bite that leads to Lyme disease? Wouldn't that fall in the horrendous category?

He frowns and purses his puffy, pillow-roll lips. I do love those lips.

While I'm sure such a thing would feel horrendous, Lyme stats are probably tabulated separately. Given the lag time between a tick bite and the onset of symptoms. And then additional time before diagnosis and more severe illness.

The tree to his left is slathered in poison ivy vines; I tug my socks a little higher. Nelson nods approvingly. He is pleased. We are hiking the lower portion of the Appalachian Trail, grunting from blaze to blaze in northern Georgia.

Have there been any reports of hunters shooting hikers on accident? My question is a response to the large yellow sign warning hunters to watch for thru-hikers.

An impatient sigh inches from Nelson's mouth—I don't know, he admits. What if we just hike and admire the scenery?

Sounds lovely but I can't quite picture Nelson doing it. Unlike me, he lives by statistics and numbers. The likelihood of bad things happening remains miniscule in any single sample. The way I see it, the likelihood of bad things happening is massive on aggregate if you factor in all possible untoward events which may transpire. I don't wonder if bad things will happen—only which bad things, and when.

At the scenic promontory, I reach for a water bottle to moisten the desert on my tongue.

What's next? I ask Nelson, expecting a botanical marvel which only grows at certain oxygen-deprived elevations.

Hiking to the place where we can pitch our tents. Looks like it should be less strenuous—31 percent descent.

Knees wobbling like saplings under the pressure of a first thunderstorm, my mind wanders towards the unspecified 69 percent. Maybe I was a little tree in a prior life. I see myself as the little tree who tangoed itself to sleep in an illustrated storybook.

Meanwhile, Nelson seeks a wireless signal for his digital hiking navigation app. One single flicker would establish our current GPS coordinates in solid analog. The paper trail map I snuck into my backpack would resolve our digital problems in a jiffy but would create communication issues. I am too lazy to look. I would prefer to avoid Nelson's disappointment and the arrival of that shocked don't-you-trust-me look he displays on dubious occasions.

As he paces back and forth between sycamores, arm raised above his head, I discover his arm resembles a hungry insect antenna, and my love for this beast appears bigger than previously thought. My love for this creature named Nelson is nearing 81 percent, which is more than I've felt for anyone, and I think 81 percent might be the magic number—as close as it gets before feeling crowded.

The thoughts pulse past like sewer effulgent. I press my forehead into the bark of an oak tree and rub back and forth across the trunk, which probably appears looney but also deer-like. When a deer rubs its antlers against trees in a forest, the context is what we call natural. Maybe, like the deer, there is something hard in my head that needs shedding.

As Nelson turns from the signal to me with a cloud of alarm on his mostly-handsome brow, I rub a little harder. When he says, What have you done, Natalie? I gather my forehead reflects the rubbing in blotches of red.

Oh Nelson, it's nothing. A little indulgent eco-frottage. Innocent eco-affection. Nothing worrisome or commercial.

It doesn't matter if he believes given important things to consider, which our route, weather, compass points, whether green things grow on north sides in any significant fashion.

Which part of ourselves and this moment should we take seriously? My forehead burn looks like tinsel next to the more urgent stuff.

I don't think we are lost, Nelson enunciates carefully, his upper lip curling a tad. If he licks his lips odds say he's nervous.

If it weren't so hot, I'd hug him.

Because I'm fine with maybe being lost. Sixty-three percent lost is an edge of unknowingness I relish, a dish one must taste before dying, an ontological escargot. It is Nelson who prefers smaller margins.

Take the elevator arguments, for instance. Whenever we stay at a hotel, usually a Marriott, the same argument emerges. Nelson walks towards the elevators while I look for the staircase sign on the wall. Then he asks what I'm doing.

I tell him: I'm taking the stairs.

But why? he puzzles. That's eight floors to climb. It will take forever.

This from the feminist who ogles every mountain as a potential climb.

Because I like the stairs. Things happen in stairwells. A door shushes shut.

I hedge around the happening part, the truth being that stairwells scare me shitless, the hollow echo of my steps speeding up ever so slightly in that eerie neon light and no one else. Unless…

It's not safe, Nelson usually blurts. I'll come with you.

The problem that no percentage resolves is simple: I don't want Nelson to make it safe.

When I say I'm fine, his face works his way around surprise and settles into curiosity—Is this about upper thigh muscles? Ventures into speculation—I thought you were scared of bad things happening. Isn't that why you always ask me about the probability?

There is a sacrificial tone to his voice I recognize from long-married relationships. We come from long-married families which explains why we are not married yet. Not into things for the long-haul. Having witnessed the long haul, we're not daunted by the short stuff. Our pre's are extensive.

And there is a massive misunderstanding winking up from the linoleum tile between us as we stand in that familiar stand-off. There is Nelson who thinks I'm frightened and therefore unlikely to do something given a certain level of risk, and there is me, a woman who knows fear is risky and therefore interesting. Because something might happen. Because there will be a day—let's call it One Day—when something *does* happen. Because it happens to everyone. And a girl can wonder. A girl can live the rainbow spectrum of horrified and yet eagerly anticipate her turn.

MARY, AMONG OTHERS

MY NAME IS MARY. I am what is to be expected of a woman named after a pregnant virgin. I write poems about half-melted lollipops on the pavement and children who play in sprinklers.

Here's a generalization: I am lonely and unloved by neighbors, most of whom do not read poetry or recycle glass. My smile, like my breasts, is genuine and petite.

•

If I strike you as unassuming, this, too, is genuine. I do not wear clothing that catches your eye with its beach-condo bright colors. If there's shade, I'm already in it. Counting the number of words we use to avoid an in-depth explanation. Or thinking about birding and other hobbies I never developed to a point where the hobby developed into me.

A hobby adds a room to the house which makes us feel bigger. We grow into these accumulations, though bigness and satisfaction are not statistically-related. Watching birds is a way to grow outside the rooms. I'm interested in expanding like that.

Who hasn't stood in the pharmacy line longing to be noticed by a birder? A birder cocking his green cotton hat and rambling on about red-shouldered hawk migrations.

I've seen at least seven heading towards Boston, I could say.

The birder might sigh, revealing a mix of relief and elation. Sometimes I feel like a fool for caring so much about this stuff. It's awful nice to meet a fellow raptor enthusiast.

Yes, I might reply. Yes it is truly nice.

Later, I would review the imagined encounter from the safe confines of bed. Erase nervous gestures, remove the Wrigley's from my mouth, add a moustache to the birder's face, lower the air conditioning, button my undyed wool cardigan, pop a mint, realize I've lost my car keys, rewind and put the car keys in my purse so they aren't lost, and lose my place in the scene altogether.

Because my mother has been dead for a year and her widower has already found a lonely and generous female to fuck.

•

At first, he took in a stray dog. A bloodhound mix.

I'm naming him Everett, the widower announced.

It was as if he'd invited me to a baptism, the organized thrill of a special event wobbling atop the fear that it might not mean anything.

That's a great name for a dog, I admitted.

At this point, I spoke as honestly as one can speak when surprised. The dog was spontaneous, unexpected as an arbitrage between two parties who needed lawyers to uncover the hidden conflict. There was nothing to fight about, and yet the acrid odor of a possible fight lingered. It was as if we were playing a game of hide-and-go-seek with undercover experts manning the sidelines, ready to call foul.

If you see Everett around, just put him in your car and bring him back to my place, the widower instructed.

Technically, the house belonged to my mother who willed it to me, but I allowed the widower to reside in the house for an undetermined, long-term period. This side effect, the possessive pronoun, was to be expected. Grief turned up in unexpected places. I lacked the stamina to argue further, and so I agreed to retrieve the dog should he wander into my yard. But the words felt turgid on my tongue.

•

Awake past owl hours, I wrestle a childhood friend, insomnia. We go way back and then onward into heavy under-eye bags. For a little while, I was heroin chic, but even the addicts score four hours a night. I am what's to be expected of a female whose sleep deprivation surpasses the junkie's. I am what's to be expected of learning from life.

From the pillow, it is possible to catalogue all the special memories. The rich feel of darkness on adolescent skin near an open window. Mom's black ink pen slipping into the wine glass as she struggles to sneak out the back door, one hand on the knob, torso balancing books, wine, lighter, unspoken things. Somehow nothing dropped. And Mom smiled. See, everything is fine? From the window I watched the cigarette light her face, like a candle beneath an icon. Pen dipped into her mouth, the taste of wine—I saw this moment, how she loosened, and how she stole it from the house with its worries and demands. I needed so much from her that stealing those moments back— spying, collecting, tucking them away for myself—barely sufficed. How many times did I watch her? From behind closet doors and under beds, her face absent in thought, wandering off. Once when she stepped into the and inched back against the enamel, that instant when a beloved descends into all the words you've built around them. All the walls and the towers, no match for a sigh and a bubble.

I am awake amid an ocean of pillows and a husband who snores like a sixteen-axle truck.

This is not surprising. I am not a sudden dog looking for a loving home. I am not a nurse reaching for a widowed apple.

I am what's to be expected of a female who journals Hugh Everett's Many Worlds theory on quantum mechanics. Many Worlds theory fascinates me. I like how its rumbles are easy to switch on and off, to slip from one world to another without disappearing.

This World is one in which Mary's mother is baking blueberry cobbler from scratch. This World is one in which Mary's sister did not expire behind a green metal dumpster after being raped by a white supremacist.

This World, the one where Mary's sister was born yesterday, cannot hold a woman without bearing false witness against her. One sister makes room for another. But no one ends or disappears. No sun gets snuffed.

•

In the morning with its bagels and French pressed coffee, I am the woman whose husband cheated on her with his Vacation Bible School intern. Something has ended, not a person but an object.

Mary's sister is not the same since her contact with the white supremacist. I did not believe murders existed offscreen. The word Neo-Nazi sounds romantic if you ponder it.

The new man wears Italian leather moccasins. I am his wife but not the same wife. My eyes inspect the tile when he asks me about the faculty party. Eyes check carpet for lint as I remind him it's on the kitchen calendar.

The calendar is the same mountain panorama of twelve American landscapes.

New wife does not avoid new husband. New wife kindly redirects his attempts at intimacy which, if accepted, would force new husband into quandary and therefore sins of omission.

How does a cockatoo sound?

New wife smiles at the thought. She has no tolerance for lies.

Is this a lie? old husband asks.

No, I think.

Are you sure! Have you checked?

Why would I check? And how?

Compare two versions for verisimilitude. I don't know, honey, but I like second opinions. A human should question what seems natural to her. Often it's not.

New wife is glad to be rid of the cat and its predatory yowling. She likes how the rooms of the house have filled with sharp edges overnight.

Old husband suspected Mary was having carnal encounters with the driver from the monthly veggie co-op.

Him? Really? With all that rosacea?

No, the driver was not Mary's type. He liked to strike up conversations about terns and sparrows and winged creatures which lived nowhere nearby. Foreign birds, too little to latch.

Old husband created the possible adulteress in great detail, down to doggy-style sex in the driver's van on Thursdays.

He believed he knew beyond a doubt. Belief at such high octave is hard to discern from disbelief. Both are noisy, are prone to over-loud articulation.

•

My name is Mary. I am what you might expect of a girl who flirted with goth. Old husband did not believe he was betraying me by sleeping with some skittle. He was the adulterer he disbelieved.

Conversations about the skittle resembled analysis of Santa Claus and tooth fairies without whiskey.

I am a good wife when New—and a resilient wife on the second round of existence. Tougher than the green sponge in my hand that promises to scour any grease stain. But also sweeter than the peach cobbler at Morrison's Cafeteria, the sticky corn syrup version.

Once upon a time I baked with sugar, but now I use Karo. My brother drank it once thinking it was vodka. This was an accident. Accidents were common in the Jablonski family.

Mary Jablonski? Gas station clerks scowled and packed snuff deeper into their lips, pronouncing my name like fresh spilled ammonia.

We married under a magnolia. I knew its limbs were too frail to hold us together.

Jablonski is Polish.

Magnolia is south of the Mason Dixon.

His great aunt from Tallahassee adjusted her Ray Bans.

Jablonski? Is that Russian?

Sure I said. Kudzu and kipper snacks. A time when I wanted to learn more about myself. See the girl as they saw her. Keep the beat of magnolias alive for however long was left.

In less than two years I went from Russian to Bosnian to Jewish to Hungarian to Macedonian.

Poland was out of bounds. The truth was foreign to the average Alabama eye. Tomato blights and droughts took up our free time. Water wars with Georgia.

The nice man I married, his name I married into. Smith. Mary Smith.

Nursery rhymes I memorized for the children. But all the mystery was gone. What is magnolia apart from the wonder of hours lost between branches and trees impossibly tall, not what one would call current. Old-fashioned gangly trees with boils and cankles.

New husband tracks new wife in the garage.

What are you doing?

Looking for wood glue.

Well why don't you ask before rummaging through my stuff?

I ask for wood glue. He says we don't have any. It's time to run an errand. At the Home Depot, the colors of paint sound like storybook pictures. The check-out clerk offers a compliment concerning my well-behaved children.

It's a fluke, I say carefully.

First time I've used this word in public. First time you use a word, and it feels artificial as a telegram. I suspect people don't mean what they say in those telegrams where each word is capitalized.

You should see them at home.

Clerk laughs and fans her brow with one of those mug shot newspapers featuring young girls on the cover looking caught. Jailbait sells. Home Depot would know.

What's that on your neck? she asks.

I pay by check.

Oh I don't know. But I can imagine it looks like a love bite. A hickey sucked hard. A relic of days with old husband.

It's not what you think.

I say this to the clerk.

I say this again when I get home.

I say this to the man so many times it feels like a hymn.

It's not what you think. Maybe it's a hymnal.

At which point the litany becomes obvious: Standing here near the stove minus a spatula but up to the same old earnest attempt to communicate, and you in the chair with those pinched lips possibly listening. If you unpinch those ears and loosen those lips and stop staring at the Elvis poster.

There's this surly event known as quantum transition when a person looking splits into two selves, one sees the particle, the other whole. Or something.

You stare at me like you can't decide which.

Aren't I the woman near the stove? Do I look like any girl you remember meeting at the creek? Mary Jablonski. With a lisp and a pocket of lucky pebbles.

New wife to old husband: Aren't I the woman you promised too much?

New wife to new husband: Do I still remind you of Sigourney Weaver in the movie based on the Mamet play? The really twisted one?

Mary Jablonski to Mary Smith: You used to love Kit Kat bars and uplifting Vivaldi.

Mary to that man: Mirror mirror on the wall, do unto her as you've done to us all.

FROM NOTHING TO ONE

You know who I am
You've stared at the sun
Well I am the one who loves
Changing from nothing to one
                              —Leonard Cohen

WOMAN RENDERED
SPEECHLESS BY SUNSET

THE ROSY PINK SUNSET light, like a knife against my throat, a color which keeps me from speaking. I am mute as the United Nations before an atrocity—the sight minus the sound-effects which lead others to listen. Not once in my life have I turned to speak and heard a lover, friend, or other say: Hark.

If there was a headline above me, it would read: woman rendered speechless by sunset.

If this was a French film, there would be no subtitles. The lack of white moving words would serve the right silence. I think silence sounds the same in French and American—silence is the same nerve in any language.

Randall sits in the den with his brother and a few odd relatives, a handful of wives who may be mistresses part-time, but also the bald uncle from New Jersey.

Sometimes I don't know what this country is coming to, he announces.

Then everyone returns their attention to the screen which displays a parade, and it is as if he hasn't said what he said. It is often like this with the TV, and then no one saying anything. Not what he said, at least.

But silence eludes us. No silence because the announcers are rousing watchers to admire the floats—look at that purple feather boa, and how many birds does it take to make a boa like that—and the adjectives are vivid, almost verb-like, followed by exclamation points. In a sense, the silence stolen by the parade in some podunk, rural town diminishes the power of the sunset which rests like a half-melted lozenge on my tongue waiting to be explained. A sunset alternates between lozenge and blade in less than an hour. Yet nobody mentions it.

I stand near the kitchen window doing two things: watching the lawn change colors and pretending to watch the lawn change colors. At one point I find myself perched inside the strange instant betwixt watching and pretending. Time is a smooth surface rumpled by speed-bumps. Like any well-traveled road, the present has its tire-filled ditches, its liminal parts.

In the den: So Randall, those leaves could use a good raking-to. Maybe you ought to invest in a blower.

In response, a surly grunt from Randall. A change of channels. Not anything he says aloud.

Because: he did not buy the leaf blower like he promised three weeks ago. Whatever he bought was not a leaf-blower. Whatever he did was not keep a promise.

The leaves clutter the sidewalk and the gutters as they did in the old days. I remember my childhood—its pink oak dusk. Those neighborhood boys with baseball caps and bottle rockets. The reckless haste of half-hidden hand-jobs in janitor closets at the Methodist church. The scent of fresh sperm and fake leather hymnals. One can't help but conclude a vast amount of current kink arose from that innocent combination.

The sunset wanders into its usual oranges and gold. Pink is the shortest part. Silence opens like a fruit bowl waiting to be filled for display. Until Marjorie muddies it up. Her high, shrill giggle streams into the kitchen where I can almost see her lady-fuschia nails brushing across a man's arm as she lowers her gaze. That Marjorie and her fool-flattering approbations. We might have been bosom buddies if it wasn't for the way she pretended to love football. Or the way she took Randall's side about guns and hunting decoy decor in the foyer.

One trusts a woman like Marjorie like one counts on the sun to stay pink—for one split second—and then, not at all. I keep a tight lid on expectation given contrary physical evidence. See, I know for a fact that Marjorie isn't half the onslaught she lays on so thick and creamy.

It must have been last Easter because the bunny displays were out. I stopped by the auto parts store for a battery. At the time, Marjorie was still working her way up from a cashier position. There was a man in heeled boots at the counter asking about windshield wipers for his truck, but I could tell Marjorie's heart was not in it. Her hands fluttered round her head like game hens, but the voice came across flat, disenchanted. The man clicked his boots on the tile floor—he was trying to buy something, he was ready to lay money down. But not Marjorie. She hid her face behind a brochure to avoid paying down the exuberance of her high-plucked eyebrows.

I suppose there's no use in confusing a client. He has a right to expect good service, but the smile part is context-dependent. Either way, I don't recall if the man bought much, but I pity the fool who buys into Marjorie.

I pity the fool I married, too. A man who can't find the silver lining or the fleece in adjacent silence. The noise he needs blaring through every room in the house so he doesn't have to notice walls change colors.

It may be consolation to believe we belong to some fiction. Consolation or curse. Terrorist or freedom fighter.

Any more Havarti in there? Randall calls.

I haven't decided whether to stay silent. There's no

Havarti left, but I can't make that more interesting than the screen.

•

Randall and I met on a flight from Tripoli to Beirut back in the 1970's when there was still a good reason to study anthropology. Field work was the call of the times. As soon as the drink service began, two men in black masks and a woman with a scarf tied across her face announced the plane was hijacked. At the time, Randall was the man across the aisle wearing frayed jeans and thick angle eyelashes, a prayer rope over his collar. The silence was loud as a ferris wheel—all the screams we held in for fear of drawing attention. Only Randall seemed to exist outside the horror and excitement, his eyes following the terrorists up and down aisles.

It struck me as polite and impossible when he raised his hand and waited to be called on. A terrorist spoke in clipped foreign syllables sticky as Arabic or Hebrew, the intonations not yet colored by years of CNN.

Yes, Randall said. I was just wondering if there was anything I could do to help speed this show along. I have a harmonica, for example. I could play a few tunes while you freedom fighters decide what to do next. If the passengers get bored, they are likely to distract you from whatever your mission. If you have a mission, that is. Maybe go on and say it and I'll pick up from there.

The clicking noises from the airplane cockpit, the unguised horror on the faces of passengers, the dimmed aisle lights which added to the ambiance we would later recognize as classic terror scene from television. It was as if Randall already knew.

Yeh, a German accent, a casual nod.

The female holding her knife in the air and making chic,

suggestive slashing motions as the short terrorist said: We are a group fighting for the freedom of Konigsberg which must be returned to its rightful German owners. We are the LAK or Liberation Army of Konigsberg. If you follow instructions, no one will die. This is merely a hijacking for money and weapons. We are— The man blanked.

Fuck Kaliningrad! the woman shouted from beneath her muffled mask, knife in the air.

Yes, nodded Randall. Why don't we fuck Kaliningrad!? And with this he began playing a melange of Mississippi blues on his harmonica as the terrorists whispered happily amongst themselves.

The expression *New World Order* had not yet reached its zenith as a catch-all, so there was no way to describe how it felt to be serenaded by an American on a hijacked flight to Beirut. But there was an aura of revolution and super-stition in the air—a certainty that whatever came to pass would be fantastic and entertaining for viewers at home.

I had read somewhere that both Hannah Arendt and Emmanuel Kant were from Koenigsberg, the German city which had become Kaliningrad after the Soviet invasion. Also that Kaliningrad was home to the Baltic fleet and fancy Soviet submarines. I imagined the furor of smolder-ing *heimat*.

As for you, Manly Man of the Dartboard in a Small Town Bar, I think we've all heard your opinion on hostage situations before. Keep that glossy hairless chest to your-self. Keep that flag in your pants. I have never been the kind of woman that gets hungry for a Manwich.

Our landing in Beirut was uneventful. We were not even dehydrated or famished because the terrorist had distrib-uted all the items from the food cart in an effort to show how nice life would be in the Republic of Konigsberg.

Do you have reservations at a hotel with cable? I nodded.

Randall had told me his name as we ate crackers. He wanted more SkyMiles. He wanted to see Maronites. He wanted to be part of something big that hadn't happened yet. But he didn't want to be part of Vietnam—no, he had protested with Dr. Spock at the capitol—because he preferred not to take sides in other folks' wars of liberation.

If you take a side, it always looks wrong on TV, and there's just no way to recover from that, he said.

You can stay in my hotel room.

If there was such a thing as a hero, it was Randall, the bard of the LAK hijacking, the mystic of international flight space.

I remember the way he looked from behind on the balcony as he smoked bidis. The sharp red of his hair, the silence he never let happen. And when he turned, the sunset shrouded the cityscape in a damask fog, a haze of singular pink. At this point, I was already naked.

Randall nodded, his hair the flame of flowers.

I think this looks just about right, he said.

It was the light.

No, it's the noise. I like to know the noise that's coming. This will be good noise, he said. This will be an ongoing level of good noise. It's the noise and the silence and the sunset. Terrorists or freedom fighters. I guess you know what when the light feels right.

TWO FACES

1. Funny Face

He was telling a joke about passports which loosely incor-
porated certain immigrant elements waiting outside Home
Depot at six AM. His friend laughed because it was funny,
but the woman who was supposed to be in the den helping
the children did not believe they were really laughing. They
were making laughing sounds and wearing funny faces, but
the noises coincided with a sense of the familiar. You two can
laugh and say it's funny but only because you've both seen
the man outside Home Depot. She wishes the men were
honest enough to admit the familiar touched them in a way
they couldn't describe and so they laughed instead because
laughter is by its nature indescribable. The best example she
found was pulling down her pants and mooning them. Her
husband laughed, but his friend blushed because the naked-
ness startled him. See, she said. One of you laughed because
it was familiar, and the other just cringed, but no one could
say this was funny. She made a funny face to be specific.

2. Serious Face

He found the letter she'd written to a lover she imagined
when she was pregnant and reading Margaret Atwood.
There was no limit to the Atwood she read in bed. She said
the letter wasn't written to anyone that existed, and if he'd
read these books about pregnancy, he would know it was
common for lovers to appear and disappear during periods

of prolonged bedrest. He wanted to know why she was laughing. What was funny? Was this her version of pop culture? And why did the pillowcase she embroidered for him suddenly look like a parody? She said it was normal to doubt your spouse when you found a suspicious letter but only if you were already prone to suspicious mindsets and revisionist thinking. A serious man wouldn't take this seriously. A serious man would laugh at what wasn't true. Sure—there was a racy letter which involved black leather halters, but she hadn't expected milk to leak from her breasts at Starbucks either.

SOMETHING ABOUT
SUNSHINE IN SCRAPYARDS

for Cameron

IN THE GRAVEYARD FOR old cars, you scour the dashboards for habits. Things which die hard decompose slowly. Cellophane stacked in passenger-side doors, empty cigarette cartons, a receipt, an unsent letter—material which began but never got around to happening.

Grant leans against a broken hubcap, his cheeks flushed pink, a just-slapped blotch typical of fair complexions. He watches you with half-lidded eyes, but you are not interested. There is more to find in the sunlit scrapyard than teenage excitement. Flecks of orange paint on the ground. Small metal screws and thingamabobs. His hand is on your ass, but you clench against it. A flex-off.

Come on, he whispers low, a gravel-eating voice, guttural.

You try not to laugh at him. Stifle the giggle at a boy who is embarrassed and accelerated at the same time. The hot stench of summer-warmed rubber.

Not now. You try to crack the window—to jimmy down the glass so you get inside the door. Help me, you warn. As if.

He blushes again—and stiffens his shoulders. I will if you will, he says. I'll help you if you help me. Strawberry blonde eyebrows edge towards the backseat. Something about a late 60's model and pleather seats. They used leather back then.

Fine, you grant. All you want is to get inside the car.

Grant's arm thickens in impatient grappling, veins rising like rivers on a museum map—the topography of teenage muscle, what a brochure might call the interactive version. Watch and wait.

The window shimmies down far enough so he can unlock the door. A click, the groan of metal on metal, an angle opens onto the scent of old carpet and spilled soda.

You shove past Grant towards the glove compartment. There is the perfect unlocking sound, a few yellowed road maps, a silver tire gauge, two pink rubber bands, a neoprene sewing kit, one single nickel gunked with brown. An inventory, at best.

Grant toys with the tire gauge and slips it inside his pocket. You shrug and stare at the space missing a steering wheel, but you feel Grant looking. You feel his restless, revved-up gaze. The urge for fireworks.

Remember the time when we spent seventy dollars on fireworks at that roadside stand, and most of them didn't work?

He nods slow, a smile creepy as syrup across a diner.

You think maybe if you get this part over with, Grant won't be distracted. You think maybe his attention will focus on helping you find the right story. A story worth writing.

Climbing over is easy. Panties slip down faster than PTA handshakes. Lean back and he knows the next part. Naked skin sticks to the backseat, and motion sounds slurp. Grant rubs his thumb over your belly-button like he can't believe there are junkyards and naked bodies who want it.

The unzip is brisk, his bottom facing the roadway eight hundred feet away, and you doubt drivers will see much. Motion faraway is always a bird opening her wings— always an animal going somewhere.

No worries, you whisper, but hurry. The rush is not the same wanting, but the wanting hovers there between you, however shaded.

When he glides in, you feel his knees tremble, the throttle of a key igniting the spark which starts combustion and sets off an engine. The sweat on his shoulder is acrid as nasty uncle T-shirts, but you lick it anyway because he's running you so hard your butt lifts from the seat. The smacking sound is your response to his key.

It sounds like clapping. In kindergarten, everyone clapped at the end of a story. Clapping and thanking the teacher for reading.

From the road, birds flutter and set off in flashes.

All adrenaline and smoked-up cigs, smacking and guttural groans, the coming explosion, the mounting noise and speed and signs you don't bother to read. Grant knows where you're going with his eyes closed. You can barely keep up. When his shoulder bangs into your jaw, you stop it with teeth. A hard bite. Like a woman sinking incisor into a fresh apple. One time and the boy is sunk. Grant moans like a dying heifer and liquid slicks your upper thighs. His weight covers you—pins you to the place he wanted.

You bite him again. He shudders. Convulses.

Get up, you shout. Because this is not a story. Sweat and smoked metal is no story you want to tell. What you do with Grant is pure mechanics en route to more interesting destinations. The sun burns your eyes.

From the road, a little girl who lost a front tooth points towards the stacked metal cars. Mommy, she says, oh mommy there's a really pretty bird down in that car. One day the little girl will develop wings, and all birds will become the same: a handful of tousled feathers, a head looking away.

G-D's OPEN WOUND

THERE IS NO G-D apart from G-d, and this is true in any language which permits G-d to serve as both subject and object in a sentence. This is when televangelists describe tsunamis or sex addiction as the work of Satan. This is true when a little girl chews on the end of a loosening hair braid. There is no G-d apart from G-d, I promise her.

There are masks we pour over G-d to play funny human games. Halloween is not a game, and it started as something serious, though it feels like a game where tricks are sticks and treats are carrots. Halloween is not a game so much as an education, a consumerist socialization. There are fabrics and flags and intercontinental ballistic missiles, but no G-d besides G-d and no terror in his name.

There are Hummers parked in garages, but there are no Hummers parked in garages on the side of town where landfills are re-permitted. There is a gentrified downtown strained by the muscles of growth and development. The gentrification is what marketing professionals describe as a soft open. A new landfill to house the waste from the thriving megachurch side of town is carefully planned to coincide with the boundaries of those who have not. There are many sides of town but no G-d apart from G-d and no name that divides G-d into separate pieces.

I grew up in the part of town that is currently occupied by Whole Foods and Old Navy. I grew up outside the parts into which we now divide the town.

On Sundays, I attend a mid-size church for whom the Scriptures stays silent on gay marriage. Facelifts and tummy tucks perch atop red velvet cushion pews as the communion tray scurries from hand to hand. We have outgrown the communion line, and the sermon has grown longer to replace it.

Mrs. Dulfus is gratified when the blessed grape juice tray pauses and the tiny clear plastic cup passes her lips. She likes her house (and the other two houses), but gratification she reserves for the discovery the church elders switched from 20 percent juice mix to 45 percent blend. Because G-d's people deserve the best. The best fruit from faith's wine and more as well.

I know Mrs. Dulfus from the brief span of time in which I performed the role of part-time accountant for elderly females who imagined themselves widows by husbands who were no longer there.

Mr. Dulfus disappeared into the shroud of early-onset Alzheimer's. There was no shortage of purse-sized Kleenex when Mrs. Dulfus described how much life could resemble death. He used to play golf every Saturday and now he can't pay attention to ESPN or CNN, though he enjoys spending time with his grandson, watching Baby Einstein videos.

It is a relief to be done with accounting. I never knew what to say when upstanding citizens revealed their financial undergarments and then asked for my opinion, the professional stance on nudity was a series of numbers I could not relate. There is no G-d apart from the one who forgives me—no G-d apart from a subject who waits.

Before my mother died, she sent a postcard from Greenland, but the stamps were written in Latin. I miss you she wrote. You could still go back to school and become an actuary. The actuaries walked away with half the investments she left behind, but the going was legal, and the walking was a bluff because they lived in Oregon. If I had followed Mom's advice, I could have inherited her investments. Instead, the faraway actuaries added sun porches to their lovely homes.

The problem is that people are not honest.

If people have never been honest, that does not mean there is no problem. It only means the problem is bigger than one girl can imagine alone.

I am dating a man who is a devotee of absolute honesty. You know him by the way he signs his full baptismal name on paper checks. You know him when he doesn't thank waiters who forgot honey mustard. You wonder what kind of woman would date such a man. I can't fill in the blanks of the type you already suspect.

We sit on the dock at sunset while the boy curdles yellow foam. Gregory sits in a wood chair on the dock, a self situated slightly off-kilter. He is tired of being honest and unappreciated. I pretend to understand the compass points reflected back. It is the third time we have tried orienteering. Gregory rumples his thinning hair and watches the water, though what he sees is not what shines back.

I want to tell him the reflection is a vending machine, but is that true? He doesn't trust his judgment right now. A sun sets, but who can say it's the end of a day and not the beginning?

Who can say what we've been sold on this scene?

Tenderness covers his eyes like canine cataracts. But tenderness is not a true or false statement. Tenderness is a perspective we can't prove.

Gregory says it's the culture that causes us grief. Americans root for the deceivers, the currency of future redemption narratives for Lifeway shelves.

We don't like victims, he says, because they tell the truth

and nothing else. It's the deceivers who get the last word. It's the deceivers who tell us the meaning of the story. The victim should have known better.

There are no stones to skip because we are on a dock. There is nothing we can do with our hands except hold them back from doing other things.

It looks like rain is coming, Gregory says.

Yes, there is possibly rain on the horizon.

Maybe we should walk back to our bikes, he says.

If you'd like to start walking back, I'm sure the bikes will be there.

Gregory's cheeks turn pink—why do you sound like a robot?

Do I sound like a robot? Why?

You would fail the Turing test with this cheap template matching, he shouts.

He is honestly rather angry and committed to absolute honesty in conveying this. I wonder if a marina is its own part of town. I wonder if I sound like a robot—if all females who have sex with honest men sound like robots. Is a robot my response to Gregory?

Though he eyes the thick silver hammerhead formation, Gregory does not make an effort to stand or leave. There are worse things than getting soaked right now. Alternately, there are better things than staying dry. But he isn't giving any feedback about what he wants to avoid or experience. Best to wait and watch.

A stateless conversation is filled with stateless remarks. For a remark to be stateless, it demonstrates no connection to previous remarks or social cues. It exists out of context.

Hey, look at that bat is not a stateless remark if we are both on the dock when the bat marionettes past, nearly hitting Gregory's shoulder. There is a shared context in which this remark would be rooted in our shared experience. There is—this.

I love you, sweetie, on the other hand, could be worse than a Mexican migrant. There is no context for that remark in our current state.

A relationship is not a context which renders *I love you, sweetie* un-stateless. Sure there are appropriate moments for such words, but this is not one of them. This is insufficient.

Besides, Gregory is brutally honest and therefore unlikely to express a sentiment he cannot falsify. A statement cannot be true unless it can also be false. You cannot *I love you, sweetie* unless you can *I don't love you, sweetie.*

It seems the *sweetie* part is the problem. Take away *sweetie*, and Gregory could say, "I love you." Unless he is indifferent. Given the coming storm, I suspect indifference is involved.

One way in which computers avoid being found out is by inserting sudden verbal abuse into certain conversations.

Gregory says, You are acting like a robot.

If I was a robot, I could hide my machine head with: Fuck you. Or, you're a smug and insolent prick.

If, however, I am myself, namely, a female who does not want to hurt an angry man, then I am more inclined to say, How am I acting like a robot? This is called active listening.

To Gregory, this is template matching, evidence of my robot self.

I think we should probably head back, but saying this sounds too robotic, and there is no G-d apart from G-d and no wound that cannot be covered with linen or a kiss.

In a nice but not ostentatious part of town, there is a little girl named Sally who thinks I am her mommy. There is no moment between us that comes out robotic. There is a worried line between her brows because mommy got wet.

There is a pale gray coverlet and a panda named Toronto and a story I must speak before she goes to bed. There is a story she needs to spread wide open. There is a feeling called love in her head.

This is not near the landfill, but the landfill is not far either. This is true, though it begs the question of being honest. G-d's open wound pulses inside my chest. You know what it means. You've settled for less.

DEAR COMMITTEE FOR THE SOCIALIZATION OF ILLEGAL IMMIGRANTS

I RECEIVED YOUR LETTER two months after marrying Mike. The letter was printed in blue Courier font, and the graphics were abysmal.

To get a sense of the writer, I checked the signature. I do that with books as well—Google the author before reading the book. This is largely to keep from over-empathizing with pedophiles and CEO's. I don't let myself read books by pedophiles and CEO's because I get sucked into anything with a heart.

The letter was signed The Committee for Socialization of Illegals, but there was no signature above the name. There was no single individual willing to take credit for this letter. It was like a lottery ticket in that way.

Beneath the unsigned committee signature, there was the following sentence:

```
We pride ourselves on being the friendly
arm of your national security apparatus.
```

Both the signature and sentence were preceded by the word *Sincerely*.

In Romania, no honest person uses *sincere*. It is a political word bandied by bigwig communist officials and their capitalist successors. Your willingness to use such a loaded, dishonest word discouraged me.

I didn't want to read the letter unless it asked me to fill out another form in which case I had no problem filling out forms and paperwork. But I didn't want to read the letter.

After boiling a pot of skullcap tea, my nerves were soothed, and I was ready.

```
This short guide is intended to help
you build a brighter, better self in
accordance with current regulations and
expectations regarding citizenship.
```

This sudden outburst of optimism lifted my spirits. Had I misjudged you? Had I presumed covert action where there was mid-afternoon sunlight?

The acrid aroma of barbeque wafted in through an open window. I recalled that tender first day of school in America, how the fifth-grade faces lit the room with welcome. I was the new student whose parents had fled a communist country, flush with American dreams.

```
Obviously, you want to become an Amer-
ican because everyone on the planet
either 1) wants to become an American or
2) is in the process of being American-
ized by our markets and soft displays of
military prowess.
```

The above-quoted paragraph suggested the existence of a template—at least a measurable process known as Americanization. I Googled various combinations of your words and came up with commercials. It's hard to know what you want if it's left abstract.

For example, can I be an American like Harriet Tubman rather than Abigail Adams? More woodsy than parlor type. More wild than billboard-tamed.

What I like about becoming an American is the hope of being myself. This self includes another language, a native tongue, in which cabbage is boiled on the stove and adults gather together in kitchens to drink home-brewed plum brandy and tell foreign stories. In these stories, there are no winners or shiny new Toyota SUV's. In these stories, *integrity* is a word used to describe those who spent time in jail, and *courage* bears no relation to Iron Bowls or police uniforms. *Courage* is a word reserved for refuseniks.

As for soft displays of passive-aggression, I felt that prowess did not deserve mention. I felt that prowess was a personal problem best left to licensed therapists.

At this point, I drank an energy drink and practiced deep, cleansing breaths in the kitchen before reading the rest of the letter.

We take this as an assumption, and we hope that you appreciate the time and dedication applied by our panel of experts to the creation and propagation of this nation-loving pamphlet.

I admire your assumption. Governments socialize children into these assumptions during a class called History. I've never met a government that didn't.

In Romania, we read the founding fathers, including Marx, Lenin, Stalin, Ceauşescu. I've never met a government with founding mothers. Females tend to be limited by the demands of their mammary glands.

I remember reading an article in which Lenin waxed poetic about Taylorism and the rise of mechanized factories. Like your capitalists, Lenin loved industrialization. He loved forcing women into the workplace to maximize production quotas.

If women complained, Lenin said freedom was not for everyone. Give a woman a job and she'll whine about the bread lines. Give a woman freedom and she'll demand a leadership position.

My parents whispered about Lenin. They took his words as permission to emigrate to the capitalist West.

In America, I learned that Lenin was a communist who could not resemble a capitalist given what was described as the Cold War. Communists and capitalists were opponents in this war. My body was divided between two sides of propaganda: consumer-topia and commie-heaven. In the years when all my T-shirts pledged allegiance to Coney Island, I sought refuge in an imagined heaven of freaks, geeks, and mermaids.

In high school, my P.E. coach and A.P. Government teacher used me as a textbook example of why communism fails. If communism was perfect, why had my parents defected? If communists were such great gymnasts, why couldn't I serve a volleyball?

In this sense, I was an exemplary American. A heavy piece of ammo to lob leftwards.

```
We encourage you to read these short
lessons aloud with your family and dis-
cuss the appropriate teaching fables
included in each section. Possible
discussion topics include how char-
acters behave in an appropriate or
```

```
inappropriate manner, and what would
be the American thing to do in given
circumstances.
```

But your envelope did not include the alleged pamphlet so it is impossible to discuss missing teaching fables.

I should add that Mike and I don't have children. We have no plans that include children, since I have yet to meet a nonparasitic baby.

Given my utter distaste for reproduced humans, I am surprised by your family values, values which force baby-hating females like myself to give birth. Since abortion has become more difficult to procure—and since my birth control stops working when mixed with antibiotics—I plan to handle my next pregnancy cheaply. If the line shows up blue, I will procure pain medicines and/or crack cocaine and proceed to consume copious amounts. In this way, the child I am forced to bear will be taken away from me.

This child perhaps will be a crack baby. I've heard good things about crack babies. My sister-in-law is a yoga instructor and a former crack baby. My husband might have been a crack baby if they'd tested him. I have nothing against crack babies or the countless junkies who chase butterflies in the park.

The American thing to do is wait for my pamphlet. In high school, the American thing to do was bubble-gum-flavored lip gloss and Noxzema. The pimple on my nose confirmed my classmates' suspicions. American girls grow up, but aliens only grow into bigger, less palatable aliens.

After watching late-night crime shows, I realize there are multiple ways to kill a variety of innocent humans. Given such diversity in the killing arena, it strikes me as strange that there's only one way to be a true American, and that involves being born in the United States. If late-night crime shows and murders remain more creative than your Committee, I foresee a dull future for the *corpus Americanus*.

I wonder how long I will wait for my alien pamphlet. I wonder how many parades will pass by before I purchase a pair of bobby socks.

```
In a democracy, such discussions are
critical in allowing others to form
opinions and viewpoints. At the end of
the day, however, there is only one
right answer—and only one way to do
things the American way. We hope you
enjoy your journey as an illegal alien.
And we wish you a glorious and legal
future here in the United States of
America.
```

Other than a tiny flag sticker, the letter was a single piece of paper in an envelope. There was no phone number I might call to inquire about the vaunted pamphlet.

Some mornings I wake up wondering if the mail-person will deliver a pamphlet from The Committee for Socialization of Illegals. But most mornings I am realistic about the inefficiency of committees and go about my day as planned.

As for the tiny flag sticker, I wasn't sure where to put it. I gave it to Mike because his native-born Americanism has been raised knowing what to do with cheap stuff.

Dear Committee, Dear Readers and Note-takers for Said Committee, Dear Historians Attached to the

Committee for the Socialization of Illegal Aliens, Dearest Human Being Wearing a Flag on Your Lapel, I need to be honest about something.

After the 1989 revolution, Romanians shared scissors to cut the communist insignia from the red, yellow, and blue national flag. My parents made us watch on TV. Hundreds and thousands of Escus. Perhaps I was scarred by the sight. The only flag I can wave is one with a hole carved in its center, a holy flag, a few colored stripes of fabric with the face of a single person peeking out.

Sincerely,

A hyphenated girl from Alabama who can't wait to 1) read that pamphlet and 2) watch the demise of fracking

A SPORT WE USE
TO PASS THE TIME

WE DRIVE ACROSS A bridge intended for shepherds. The shame of our un-village manners forces the laughs from our throats—the ha ha ha how funny. The crossing is something we manage, a trick we pull, a ruse rather than a foolhardy accident, which comes from fiddling with the radio en route.

In the village, there are no billboards to relieve the tension. No women in impossible pumps leaning forward with that look of breathless astonishment, the mock-innocence you know what she means while little kids in the backseat hardly notice. No billboard face to kiss the boo-boos. No breasts to make it better. All my metaphysics come out frail and commercially-driven.

I'd hate to be a virgin again, Ralph says as a young female in black wool pants and boots guides three cows across the street.

What does beef have to do with virginity?

I wasn't thinking about beef—really. It's the milk, I guess. The cow milk. And the girl.

The radio jumbles the emanating moo sounds, the cows posing as backlit silhouettes, their lips cracked open, soundless.

I hated being a virgin from the moment I first heard the word *hymen*. The word bothered me so much—hi, men! I couldn't wait to get rid of it.

He clucks his tongue thoughtfully. I think girls like to

stay virgins. I slept with several girls who lied about being virgins. Maybe they thought I couldn't tell the difference.

But you could?

Of course. It was obvious. But hard to explain.

Did you confront the faux virgins after the fact?

Actually, I tried. I confronted the first two—look, I said, I know you aren't a virgin, you don't have to lie about it, I still had a great time—but both shook their heads and blushed and screamed tiny sharp little words of denial. Tiny no no nos. Even then, they refused to relinquish their virginity.

I feel carsick, disappointed. Ralph is not the mammal I'd imagined.

Perhaps my silence gives him the impression that he should expand on the topic—ground the topic in firm economic discussion. So he does.

To lose your virginity is like losing an investment—a value you only have once. A magic gold coin that gets you through a gate and then what? If it's value is so large as to be unexchangeable, I say virginity is a great hedge against future loss.

Don't tell me, I mutter.

Dark chocolate will solve anything from birth control to missed turns in Transylvanian villages. I think one thing and say another. Other times, I think one thing and say no thing, which leads me to think about something else I never said. And what if I had?

We stop outside a small cafe, its sign Mama's Mamaliga blazed in thick black serif font atop a plastic Coca-Cola banner, the kind you see on the fence at baseball games. The waitress ushers us inside—the outdoor seating occupied by a massive puddle.

I've always preferred Pepsi myself, I tell the waitress

who looks like an early variant of a thought inside David Lynch's head.

She doesn't acknowledge the joke. Instead, she pulls the chair out for Ralph and leans forward like a top-heavy tulip to guide his eyes through the drink menu. She giggles and laughs, and I try not to think the word *tramp*. I try not to trample her in my head, especially since Ralph squiggles his eyebrows, then laughs to fill in the silent spaces. Together, the waitress and Ralph leave no silence unfilled between them.

I'll have whatever he's having, I say.

The waitress nods and tells Ralph she be right beck vit dat beer.

It's all soft porn from here, I lament.

What? *Noooo*—her? Really? he shakes his head so slowly it feels like a time lapse shot—the extended, drawn-out *nooooo-noooooooo-noooooo* of a girl who says one thing and means another. Truth be told, Ralph's denial has all the cinematic exertion of fake female orgasm. All those *no*'s chord different.

I know what I have to do, and it's not like I haven't done it before when faced with a fembot-waitress.

Look, stare it square: the exaggerated display of porn is meant to arouse a man through flattery. Secretly, there's Ralph thinking the waitress isn't putting on a show. There's Ralph pretending to read the menu and thinking it's all for him.

Forget the historic ruins, the Roman what-nots, the conquering Huns, the Art Museum That Matters—for the purposes of foreign travel, not much of the tour guides are relevant. Because there is no place in the world you can walk ten miles without running into a bosom that wants you. The coming attraction.

I think she appreciates being treated with respect, Ralph offers, his eyes clear as good moonshine. I mean, imagine how curt and rushed her customers might be. A little courtesy goes a long way.

My eyes roll back into my head until I summon them out to face the wreck that is Ralph. It's impossible to convince him that her behavior is geared towards a male—any male—not The One on a valiant courtesy promenade before her. Because look, and look again: What's faux in the context of a good show?

Now watch and learn: I don't know Ralph, this place gives me the creeps. I'm not all that hungry anyway. Let's just go.

At first, he protests because a beer has been ordered and the waitress—no, look, you're outta there. You are walking back to the car, and he will follow. Ralph or Trent or whatever his name will follow you to the car to avoid a scene.

And then you will tell him you want a hotel. You want a bed and a bath and a glass of water and what you want most is him. Now. Credit cards and dark chocolate solving all the world's problems. Back it up with a line from William Blake: Sooner murder an infant in its cradle than nurse unacted desires. That's where this is going.

The hotel is second-rate, but Ralph has the glitter of jitter in his eyes. It doesn't take much from here. A girl knows when to spit in her hand and try to get things moving. A girl knows how to make things hurry in the same rapid motion, a coaxing movement undergirded by the clenched anxious fist. Not that it matters.

He lies like a icon beneath me—a solid piece of wood with gold glazed in the crevices where the light hits. I can feel the sweat dripping down my stomach from the fold under my breasts. I can feel the soft seer of his squint—what it takes to see me, a bas-relief. The part of him inside me and the part outside, the untidy combination of sex.

Half-conscious, I draw my fingertips along the trail of downward-sloped sweat and touch it to my lips. The same old salt.

You don't have to act things out to get my attention, he says.

But—I wasn't. Or was I? How much of this is something we want?

I'm here, he whispers from the space between the pillows.

I'm here, I reply from the air pocket above.

The fan blows the hair round my head like a cyclone, and I think for a second how we are here, joined at the hip, with all this same-old forecasts and familiar tunnel between us.

RENTAL UNITS

THE YARD IS A mess of gold and orange leaves I notice while staring out the window with a coffee mug in my left hand. Though the coffee is too hot to drink, the colors make it seem hotter. The colors make it smell scorched.

Vivi says a few leaves on a lawn does not qualify as an atrocity, but she has a high threshold for evil. She defends battered women in trials against their abusers. Mostly, she loses. The women go back to their husbands. Then Vivi comes back to the house we rent and the relationship that also feels rental.

I don't ask her to marry me anymore because I know the words she's excised from her lexicon. I know the words by heart, and *husband* is one of them. I know what husbands have done to Vivi's idea of marriage. Instead, I ask when we are going to buy our own house.

She brushes brown hair from her eyes and stares at the leaves. There is Jimi Hendrix in the background. I don't want to think about buying, she says. Vivi can't think about investments right now.

When we kiss, it's like autumn crinkles underfoot, and we are somewhere outside admiring the view of ourselves. The colors burnish the yellow freckles in her eyes. Steam from uncovered coffee makes us look good and slightly foggish.

We hold hands and wait for the coffee to cool. Today I will rake the lawn. Vivi says don't bother. She still won't buy a house. It's not about yard work anyway. Really, it's not.

The truth is that Vivi is actually blonde, and the leaves are one way for me to miss a color out loud.

She dyed her hair after the eighth husband swore to boil her in hot oil. Two months later, Vivi was fine.

Three months later, the eighth burned his youngest child in hot oil, and Vivi was not fine. The jury said it was an accident.

Vivi lost her client. The wife went back. Vivi dyed her hair after she was disinvited from the child's funeral.

•

She took a two-hour bath, and I took a two-hour bath. We did this at the same time but separately. The house has two bathrooms, but Vivi won't use the pink tile bathroom (the one with the bigger tub) because it reminds her of childhood and family prayers. Also, a pink rosary.

The water she leaves behind is tinged with brown hair dye. Vivi is a natural blonde, but there is nothing natural about husbands or handwritten death threats on Las Vegas postcards. There is nothing fair about how men get away with it.

Sometimes Vivi's face narrows like she needs to tell me something important. Like the thin face of a tulip before it cracks open wide to let light inside its bulb. I can't describe her face because the metaphor gets muddled—there is light and how it touches an open flower, but there is also the tulip bulb which is not related to electricity or innovation. There is the natural and the industrial getting mixed.

Vivi doesn't say anything when her face looks like she wants to speak through untidy metaphors. She wants to make love, and there is light in our naked bodies on the bed but not a good natural light like hair color. It is an artificial light that gets things dirty, and then she draws the bath again.

Her silence hides things including the sound of a voice asking for a towel. Her silence hides a polite please. The gurgle of running water hides her silence as well as whatever she asks when she isn't going to talk about the husbands. When she wants to admire the leaves without mentioning the house. When she thinks the mail truck will bring a green wool sweater, but it leaves a handwritten threat instead.

It's not a question of trust or anything personal. Not about me or Vivi or the house we can't buy without putting money down on what it means. Though I know it's about the husbands and their battered wives, it is hard to comb through gifts and eliminate the pink ones. Hard to hide things that might hurt Vivi when these things appear soft, pouffy, and innocent.

Today I will call her mom and tell her about Vivi's new hair color. Her mom will say we should marry and come visit soon. I will tell Vivi we talked about politics. Then Vivi will laugh and roll her eyes which means thank-you. She will bathe, and I will bathe and miss her across the house we will never buy because there are husbands. The leaves will turn browner every day. We will describe the transformation as natural.

ONE OF THOSE SINGLE-SCENE FIXER-UPPERS

ANOTHER HUMAN AT THE table would ask too much of me tonight.

I supplicate the ghosts for company.

If I were a story, I'd be one of those single-scene fixer-uppers which appear fresh & mod but are actually as ancient as a woman alone in a room with nothing to iron.

Never have I ever owned an iron.

This is not a game. At no point in life will I iron anything because I do not purchase iron-hungry garments.

To grip the handle of an iron is to tango with death. Likewise: night. Also: traffic and news headlines. Not to mention BOGO sales at the mall, or the humans sprinting resolutely round the rim of early morning parks. All these sights remind me that death is coming. Any single instant guises its arrival.

My mother confused the blood clot in her lung for sleepiness. She died in her sleep, a victim of not listening or looking askance. Persistence is an ongoing pact to listen, look, and learn. I learn little by little, flower by flower.

Learn from a rock when to keep quiet. Unless it asks.

If it asks, include every single stem.

I learned more from rocks than professors. I learned from a green Chevy truck that a car can break your back and steal two years' worth of memory from your life. Two years when you don't exist. I learned that a first kiss is forgettable given 55 MPH impact and basal skull fracture. I learned that trying an exotic cocktail drink will get you raped, which adds more chunks to what you don't remember. I learned that the face of the man you've forgotten has not forgotten you. I've learned that man could be Any Man you meet accidentally—any man who remembers something private about you. Nice for those who don't worry about how to end a one-scene story but hard if you can't help being stunned by what folks ignore. The train. The red lights. The low distant sirens. The decibel of hisses and whispers. The dark that is coming for every hopeful heart.

No matter how far you run, Reader, the slow, shrill dark will gobble you up. Inside the belly of the whale or the wolf, this is as safe as it gets. To be swallowed by a beast.

When he inhales, you inhale.

Learn to speak between breaths you share with a monster.

Memorize the bones of the arc you live inside.

WHITE TENNIS SHOES

THE GUITAR STEPS INTO the white tennis shoes on the front porch, a tune to the left of the doormat, a lullaby the girl sings to the boy she hopes will notice her. I hear what's left after two houses intervene. I hear how bad she wants him. The boy right there in the room where the same seven notes strum, but he can't hear a song except the one crocheted of lace between two parents who really loved one another, and the lace is so delicate with variations and details that he can't imagine replacing it with a thread.

The girl's voice tangles in aspen leaves but comes out slender, a slip of bubbling stream, a place where things began. Movement is a melody we invent from instants in which we perceive a pattern. The boy cannot invent. The boy sees only what came before. He cannot touch the thread she wishes to weave into a journey. He cannot see the pattern through.

•

My husband is behind the front door. Two steps behind the doormat. Missing a set of white sneakers.

He can't go anywhere without shoes. Not since the surprise of splinters.

If I had big white tennis shoes, I would avoid the undertow of family time and miscommunication removed from the freezer to thaw alongside a bottle of wine. I would never leave frozen materials on the counter and wait for the soaking.

As his wife, I sit on the front stoop and guard the sneakers he should use to escape me. The music grows tight at the corners. The night is a paper airplane half-folded, and all the motion in the world doesn't mean any of us are going anywhere.

•

I don't remember our ski trip last year. My husband retrieves the event and preserves it as a keepsake. We are not lost, he says. But who is looking?

•

He says things to keep them from being true. But he sounds so honest when he says things he doesn't want to happen even if the saying itself is a lie. Like retiring at Glacier National Park as stewards. Like a man struggles to make more and more money for forty years and then suddenly decides he doesn't need it. Suddenly decides he can work for free.

•

When we passed each other in the hall earlier—en route to children-bed deposits—he stopped me and said, if we make it to forty, the statistics of sexual infidelity dramatically decline. His eyes glowed like volume buttons on a car radio. Two volumes glowing in opposite directions. I didn't know what he meant.

Why forty? I wondered. Why stop there? What's at forty?

Well I thought it might make you happy to know. It makes me happy.

What is happy? I wondered. What comes after happy and is it well-rested?

•

These are melodies that never made it out into music because my husband doesn't appreciate mocking serious topics. It reduces his trust in me when I avoid topics by laughing them away. These are melodies that were rejected at first rehearsal. Sheet music stocked away in an old hatbox I open when the kids are at school, and the house could be anyone. The home could be a red brick woman named Margaret whose arias perfume the air whenever she opens hatboxes. The home could be a hatbox full of unsingable songs kept inside because music went out of style, and now everything is recording. Mixing or looping other people's songs in to a cacophony of Facebook pages, each one earnest, each one sure this is the real me. Or she.

•

My mother wasn't a gypsy, but that's what I tell him when I can't admit to being unserious. That's preposterous, but it's better than funny because he doesn't know what to do with absurdity since maybe it's a form of innocence he missed in his all-American childhood. We played with toy guns, he admits.

He hasn't been spiritually-certain since we left the megachurch. A good church grows. It attracts people. The church we attend is too liturgical. My husband doesn't know what to do with too much silence. Who can be silent after the Shoah? Isn't our duty to speak about important social events? Isn't it our duty to parse the news with scripture?

For a moment, he looks like a bald version of Dietrich Bonhoeffer. Or maybe more Martin Niemoller on June 27th, 1937, his hands white against the glossy wooden pulpit saying, No more are we ready to keep silent at man's behest when G-d commands us to speak. For it is, and must remain, the case that we must obey G-d rather than man. But it sounds like a pick-up line, a plea for sex, a bungled belief system. It sounds like a loose thread we can't pull into a pattern. How we want to be formed is not how forming happens.

•

I fell for him over tennis. The tennis ball he couldn't hit became the ball he sliced open with a kitchen blade. He carved it like a holiday turkey. Inside the green felt a hollow tan rubber layer about one inch thick. It looked so cheap. You aren't a loser, I wanted to say, but it was too easy to misunderstand in context. A parking lot and eyes like flints. The anti-progressive exultation of the moment when something we respect is cut apart. The kiss that follows.

You're aren't a loser, I swore. The game is cheap. Its core empty except for the shit we plant inside. A plant is a plan dyed green.

The *cantus firmus* is a yarn we've woven over, and no one can recognize it from the later layers. White tennis shoes and a song I might step into if ever I was invited. We relate in the racket, the churned noise of full-throttle family. The music is something others hear in us, but we know only the noise and clatter of frozen jawlines. The color of sun setting is more shadow than hold, more entry than anniversary.

•

A boy on the floor laughs because he can't hear what the girl who longs for him is saying. He laughs because she smiles, and the smile is easy tender to which the laugh returns or begins.

I want to help the boy see the girl even though she is a stranger possibly with lice, possibly a feline-lover who likes the idea of the boy more than the reality of what he might bring to a picture.

•

Later I go inside wearing the white tennis shoes.
What are you doing, he asks?
Those are my shoes, he says without meaning.
I'm running away. I sit on his left knee and let him touch

my back, let his hand drift down toward the haunches of hips of such scenes.

My hands smell like sage, I say, even though I didn't gather any sage or use a like-minded lotion. I let him smell my fingers.

Yes, he nods. Sage.

His shoes are too big. When I sink into his chest a tennis shoe thuds to the floor. I am a plant that doesn't grow here, but the story requires me to smell foreign and home-like. I am an herb that tastes good with turkey.

THERE WAS NO MORE
BLOOD THAN A PERIOD

What you think is the point
is not the point at all
but only the beginning
of the sharpness.

—Flann O'Brien

ILLEANA THE WEAVER

THE LITTLE GIRL SAT by the open window and watched the shepherds weave past, the scent of wool clinging to the soles of their red leather shoes, flutes bouncing like wedding bouquets—the girl watched and braided her thick, brown hair.

Mama tried to turn off the light, but it was not time.

Tell me more. Another one.

•

Her name was Illeana the Weaver. She was not a princess, but she acted like a princess because the story she recited was her own. She could speak in capital letters without blushing. Illeana watched the shepherds—her fingers had long ago memorized the motions of braiding—and never once glanced at a mirror. She didn't ask a mirror what she should do. Or ask it to confirm what she had done. Or what to become. Who to marry. She imagined these things herself.

•

No, mama. I'm not sleepy yet.

Mama's voice insisting I devise my own ending. She believed it was good to invent your own stories.

Imagination makes you stronger, she whispered.

All the girls who tend sheep are stronger. I note how they know their way through the woods at night.

But I don't want to find my way through the woods or the story. I want to sense the safety of her footsteps just in front. I want my mother's way—Illeana's.

And so I beg: I want you to imagine it for me. Tell me

the story about the crazy bumblebee. Please?

Mama stretching her legs, restless. Oh. That one? I don't remember.

My desperation for the familiar comes out in specific reminders: The bumblebee who got trapped in the nosy neighbor's purple purse?

Mama laughing and running her hand across my cheek, her mouth melting my name like a sugar-cube in hot chamomile tea.

Okay, okay… Mama relents.

Mama wagging her finger. But don't get upset if things turn out differently. I don't remember what happened in the story last time. And even if I did, it wouldn't be the same.

MOTHERS WHO DIE

AT THE FUNERAL HOME, all the flowers are fake.

I could not countenance a funeral. The extended family ached like an ingrown toenail, foreheads debauched with the aroma of Botox. An ellipses of blank stares inappropriate for the ceremonies of honest-to-goodness grief. There is no good grief. No proper punctuation. The parentheses of a hug holds us back from the statement that follows.

Seal the casket with wood glue, I told the undertaker. His shirt was a lavender bloom straight from heaven's finest arboretum. The business of death is bright colors and gaudy in person—but fancy on the next year's tax return.

•

There's an article in the paper.

The local newspaper printed an article about her two days after her death.

The title included the word beloved. Also doctor.

The active verb—dies—piddled across the page in past tense. Overall, the impression one received was definitive.

•

There's a liquor story inside extended family life.

The room smells like liquor when all the relatives arrive.

Who were you really?

I want to know the parts she didn't broadcast—the men she secretly desired while pleasing the men whom she married. The faces she added to her exquisite stews. The way night felt when it refused to wrap itself around her torso and hung loose as a sarong instead.

You're the writer, she says, but she's laughing and hard-to-say serious.

You're the writer, she says, you tell me who I was, and the story becomes who I am. The story is what's left.

I can't stand when there's something she isn't saying—a lecture from high school she hopes to bring back around, reapply in present context, the coy I-told-you-so, but not in those words.

My in-laws wave from across the room, their arms flimsy as picnic salad forks. A wave is a hi and a bye.

A wave can be frozen in time if you die in your sleep while sprawled on your stomach with a hand tucked under your cheek. A wave can be frozen in time when the coroner turns you over, and the elbow bend is the plastercast of *rigor mortis,* and no one says a word because the hand is raised high in the air, greetings and salutations, hello and goodbye, the hand doesn't lie.

A wave can be a form of life the tattoo artist inks into my body.

My body can be the receptacle for a cake I baked in secret, the cake I ate alone outside where neighbors gossiped about the daughter who looked happy—maybe she likes cake, maybe she's resilient, maybe she's got a strong faith in her Lord and Savior Jesus Christ—but whispers float across the lawn in all caps. My body can be the hidden cave where Mom is safe from prying fingers. My body can be her grave.

Did you touch the silver urn? My husband looks very uncomfortable when he asks. His face is so many colors of wave.

I laugh because it sounds ridiculous—and why on earth would I touch the urn? What business have I with her ashes unless I was planning to pilfer a cup and bake her into the cake I consume in the yard where whispers wander through ferns and dogwood shadows?

I'm serious, he sighs.

He looks very serious. He looks concerned. His concern comes across as constipation.

You should try some of this cake, I suggest, even though you couldn't pay me to share it. What business have I sharing my Mother's Heavenly Body?

It's not cannibalism because I'm not eating her flesh. I'm not eating my mother alive. I'm eating what's left of being dead.

•

It's a great idea to sew things.

I sit and wait for a friend to call because there is nothing left to sew except apron patterns. When the pain begins, I cannot believe it—Mom didn't like to sew. If she decides to meet me here near the glossy white Husqvarna, a tirade will follow suit.

The light oozes across the futon, ominous as the face of an ex-boyfriend over my shoulder looking down into a summer lake. I should be on a boat but I'm in the sewing room wishing it didn't have to be like this, and maybe it hurts because pain was part of the way we related—abdominal pain, foot pain, muscle pain, no pain, no gain—and then the pain grows bright enough to discern the shape of her hips angling forward.

Mom, I say, Mom—why do you come to me with pain?

The shadow flips a switch, a familiar inner throb, a sense in which I have misunderstood things forever. I have mistaken my mother's presence with pain, her fingertips on my temple only migraine.

•

But: sprawled on the living room floor where I am birthing pilgrims.

What will we *dooooooo?* her grandchildren wailed. They cried and played make-believe games with hand-sewn dolls. In the games, all the nice and special dolls had to die. The living room was covered in dolls that had suddenly died. The deaths were sudden and straight-faced.

I said first and foremost we needed to find the right words for this peculiar occasion.

Then I chased words through the house, up and down hallways, until the neck of the word *noooooo* quivered between my hands like an unplucked chicken. After shaking the word and slamming it against the kitchen tile wall, I removed the *n* from the series of *o*'s. There. Much better. *Oooooo* pranced through the living room like hula hoop hips, happy to sport a permit.

The dolls kept dying. Children, I said, the deathage must cease. The dearth of deathing is doing us harm.

What will we *doooooooooo?* they demanded.

We will go on a pilgrimage, I announced. We will make a map of places Grandma could be apart from inside the wolf's belly. We will find the hinterland where she is hiding and feast upon her blueberry cobbler. We will celebrate her life and maybe light sparklers.

When will we *goooooooo?* they needed to know.

I said all I could say which came out: Pronto.

•

Preparations for the voyage are underway.

I cried in the Chevron bathroom stall. I cried near the confederate jasmine vine on the left side of the mailbox. I cried in conditions of suburban sprawl. I cried on the couch, in the black bucket seat, near the diaper, halfway between the Little Free Library and a nearby house, in the funeral home parlor, in the late afternoon traffic, which turned every light orange, in the mega-box store with low prices for milk. I cried in the grass and pressed my face into the driveway pavement.

When I woke up to check if she was still dead, there were no signs of tears on my face. No concrete gravel scars.

I took this as an omen.

•

It wasn't actually an orange beach until after the oil spill.

There weren't any traditions except going to the beach in the summer so we went to a place called Orange Beach, and the only orange part were the shells strafed in leftover BP floculent.

I wrote a poem while sitting on the jetties. The poem involved noise and crunching sounds. A tooth-grinder recognizes the night before in the sound of morning cereal.

> The palm tree hustles a paved corner of paradise
> covered in condos. Sand bears evidence of palm
> fruit formed small and barely orange. A variation
> on fresh-palette peach. Then gravel gravel gravel
> more gravel plus concrete ground cover all this
> gravel is a grave. We kill the things we love if
> only to keep them. A name on the title is a deed.
> A word may be done to another. Mine.

I wanted to read the poem aloud, but the ocean raised its voice into the white foam crest , so argumentative.

If I tried to read the poem aloud, it would come out holy as cavities and flush with unmined alloys. The minerals of me are hard to hear. Metals are missing from the words I need to say. To speak is hard metal manufacturing.

•

And besides...
We didn't have any special hats, the children complained.
How can we be pilgrims without those hats?

•

There is no such thing as a zipper anymore.
Her employees wanted to look inside the casket for closure. But the casket was closed, I said. What more closure could anyone want? A closed casket doesn't mean much. The blueberry shrubs have been picked clean by birds. There is no fruit left to make a cobbler.

I wonder how she will make a blueberry cobbler for her grandchildren with this dying and all.

I read a book about how it feels when a mother dies. The book was on bestseller lists. A mother dies at least every day. Or, once a day is the death I can see coming.

The book hardly helps. Now I know for a fact that my mother will die because everybody does it.

I still don't know what to do when she dies.

I still can't believe she would go and be like everybody else.

•

Night is a mess.
Night is a curtain of hair to hide behind, a knot she'll never comb. Night is 10:27 PM when I sneak onto the red brick stoop of her house and watch the moths burn their skin on streetlights. Remember the early morning we sat here and watched the house across the street burn down. Smoke pressed through the dogwoods so slow we mistook its flumes for a litter of kittens. For something lost we could soothe with milk. Lit our cigarettes in tandem and said we were glad to not burn. Not yet.

•

People are a mess.

Her husband wants to be left alone.

But you are already very very alone, I said to myself without saying much except *ohiamsosososorryitmustbeso-hardandthensome* to the left-alone man.

•

She liked it when I didn't look messy.

In the morning I comb my hair and put on a bracelet. I wear her apple-scented perfume. I perform the role she left as co-executor of her estate. I smell like printer paper and professionals.

In Alabama a female executor is called an executrix. This is a legal term. When I inform others of my role, their eyes glaze over with soft-porn stares and Marvel comic memories. I need a better costume.

A friend hugs me hard. We are both motherless daughters. We are women whose mothers were early adopters of the technocracy known as death. We are status morticians. Our lips burn from kissing hot coffee mugs.

•

Baby steps, they say.

My sister continues to see patients. When her eyes close as she describes a recipe, I understand she cannot stand what she sees. This is why she sits on the gray linen couch while speaking. This is why her skin resembles a beautiful white tibia. She hordes bones, and soon there will be a baby. I think my love for this baby will be greater than my love for all the world's bones and babies combined. My sister is brilliant. Her love infects me like a blue-green algal bloom. We cannot consider the consequences of our toxicity on other forms of life.

•

There is a road I can't find on the map we may be making.

Where are we *gooooooing*? they chime.

They are children ever-busy clanging and chiming. They are bells, and I am the church belfry bat, mortified on the hour by what devotion does to the darkness.

Don't disrupt the darkness, I snap. The bones inside my wings carry me away.

I resolve to live for my mother. I resolve to live and then one day maybe die.

I don't want to make any promises so my words stretch through the ocean of loved one's minds like a rotten peninsula. The ground is rotten. The tomatoes we eat have grown in the ashes of other dead mothers though nobody mentions this at lunch.

I do not understand the autopsy. A massive pulmonary embolism is not a skinny-dipping internist's death. The autopsy must be referring to a rock star.

It is different to turn one's blessings into accounting statements. People who think my mom is dead don't know how she joined a four-man sailing crew in the North Sea without divulging any details until after.

•

First person to person.

In the bathtub when all the house is sleeping but you are alive and it would be so easy to suddenly drown, you recite the memories aloud.

I remember the way she smelled in her late-evening pajamas. And the thick wool socks hand-knit from Transylvanian sheep.

I don't remember whether she put salt on the sour cream she ate with midnight tomatoes. The heart beats like a drum circle in my chest. I don't remember. I don't remember.

I will die because I don't remember.

She is dead of what I don't remember.

She is dead with things I don't remember.

Head underwater and only the sound of intentional bubbles. Big, purposive breaths. I imagine how it feels for the breath to stop without fighting the stop. I am dying every single day, and Mom is the light who shows me the way.

This skinny woman in the bathtub is not a person I recognize. She is sad and mopey. She has yet to swallow the communion wafer without crying. She crosses herself and sobs in the church pew. She's the woman I think should stay home until she can get her act together enough to go out.

Get up, I scream to the self whose shoulders I'd like to shake and shake and shake. Get up and get back to living. Mom doesn't want you to die or drown. She didn't like people who wallowed.

The only wallowers she liked were painters, poets and monks. She loved painters, poets and monks more than anything else.

The woman who steps out of the tub and brushes her teeth is not me. The woman who climbs into bed and swallows two Bach flower remedy lozenges is not me. The woman who hugs and kisses Republicans is not me. The woman on the threshold of nice cotton sheets that rustle like coffins is a word that won't lay down. Me is a motion.

There is a yellow puddle of streetlight near the mailbox. I stand with my toes over the cusp of available light.

I remember other things she said, and now the pronouns are muddled. The courage with which I throttled *nooooooo* tucks the children to sleep and waits by the foot of their bed.

Come with me, I beg.

No, it snarls. Go be a big girl. Go get you some big girl boots. Go listen to country music and shoot big girl guns.

My chin drags like a badly-thrown anchor. Pieces of jellyfish arms sting my eyes. I remember things she said, and remembering turns into the game we play with ghosts. Maybe you'll write poems about me after I die, you said, eyebrows lurching. G-d, you were beautiful. Expectant.

I shrugged because two can play at the you'll-love-me-later game.

Maybe you already knew how it would feel to win. To be right forever. To be the voice we never ignored again. The sonnet behind every sparrow and sunset. A reluctant country song we couldn't stop seeking.

In this game we play with ghosts, the pot is yours. I lose but can't stop playing. Come back, mama mama mama mama. I'm going to make a ruckus and throw toddler tantrums on the street. Convince me why I should remain in the land of the living where only losers are left.

THANK OUR LUCKY STARS

A NEIGHBOR SAID WE should thank our lucky stars there hadn't been a drought this year.

I refused to consider thanking unidentified intergalactic bodies. How did she know our stars were lucky? And whose stars were the one she called our stars?

A town could not very well share the same horoscope when drivers had trouble sharing traffic lanes. We were not a sharing kind of town. College football teams estranged team spirits every fall season.

Assuming we had been more of a community than a mere town, there was no way we could share the astrological charts.

If the neighbor was a Baptist, it is possible she believed in a variant of lucky stars unrelated to horoscopes or ancient Egyptian astrologies. But then her lucky stars would belong to all Baptists including those newly-converted in Korea and Afghanistan. If she was suggesting Koreans and Afghans had not suffered a drought this year, I don't see how she could know this as a fact. Did she follow Korean and Afghan weather online? Was there a chart for global Baptist weather available to insiders?

On the other hand, if she maintained a distinction between the stars of Korean-Afghan Baptists and Alabama Baptists, this would undermine the integrity of her Baptist worldview. Even a Baptist worldview is required to include the entire Baptist world in its considerations.

I am not a Baptist, I told the neighbor. At the time, it was the only sure thing.

THE ICONOGRAPHER

THE TOUR GUIDE DISAPPEARED inside the tiny, womb-shaped chapel of a town called Domremy-la-Poucelle. It was hardly a town at all—merely a village accessed by long, silver tour buses that promised life-changing experiences to Joan of Arc fans.

Though I arrived on the morning bus as a member of Group A, my purpose was not really religious. Though I wanted to assert this distinction apart from my fellow Americans, I also felt submerged by the groupiness of things—the anonymity, the mispronounced proper nouns, the ongoing attempt to define myself as an individual in a different national context. Unlike fellow American tourists, I had come to retrieve an incomprehensible portion of childhood, the year devoted to creating a deck of cards which depicted various scenes from Joan's life. At the time, I wore braces and could barely eat steak.

When people asked, I said I was a vegetarian.

When people asked, I said they were baseball cards but not about baseball.

The context was foreign. A rumor circulated that I could read Tarot, but the rumor was false and I pretended not to notice words like Tarot in whispers.

The tour guide had hairy legs, which stood out given the sparse patchy hair-pattern atop his head. He might have been blonde as a child. At that point in time, however, he was inching into middle-age tired.

Joan of Arc was born in this hamlet and it is here, inside this very chapel, that she received her first divine revelation.

A tourist kneeled and began to pray with beads. The rest of us felt left out and slightly guilty for not bringing our own beads. The guide said beads could be purchased from the Visitor's Shop. He sighed and then trudged off to locate a priest who might relieve us of our guilt and money.

We felt inclined to spend our Euros because the exchange rate was not so hot.

Wasn't her name actually Jeanne d'Arc? I asked the guide's young assistant.

Mais oui, she replied. In French.

What's that? asked the bow-legged older man wearing a God Bless America cap. What's that you just said about Joan?

He nudged a woman to his right whom we recognized from the bus as his wife.

Joan is Jeanne in French, the assistant said calmly.

John, huh? Well, lookie-here. John is a man's name. I've been trying to explain to Sally ever since this Joan obsession got started three years ago in a hotel in Tampa. Ever since then I've been trying to make her understand that girl was trying to be a man. One of those switchers—you know, the kind that changes sex. Really popular right now in America, this switching around.

Sally ran her finger along the ledge of a small wooden pew reverently. Her eyes darted into the secret gullies and shaded corners of the chapel, which smelled garden after spring rain. The walls had been carved from dirt so we couldn't tell the church smell from the nature smell. The aromas came together in a sort of quiet harmony.

John of Arc, huh? the man chortled, his white eyebrows disappearing beneath the rim of the cap. Just think we paid all this money and came to a foreign country so a French person could tell you I was right all along, honey.

This is the window through which Joan of Arc day-dreamed as a child.

Sally's husband was thirsty. He wanted to know where he could get a decent Coca-Cola product in this church. There was a sign for restrooms, but where were the vending machines?

A priest who looked too young for his cassock stood next to the guide. The priest's hands were folded inside his sleeves like a makeshift muff.

Co-la? he smiled.

We could tell he was a gentle priest, accustomed to blessing cows and baptizing cartloads of spring peasant babies.

The priest whispered something French to the guide and both men nodded.

Then the guide nodded by himself and addressed Sally's husband: Sir, it is against the rules to wear a hat inside the chapel. If you would be so kind as to hang it from the hooks by door, the priest would be grateful.

I noticed a bird's nest in one of the windows abutting the ground which reminded me of a long-ago tornado shelter, half-submerged in dirt.

Sally's husband glanced around the room, narrowing his eyes in a search for allies.

Now lookey-here, he growled, I don't like being disrespected. Seems to me the priest could've told me that himself, man to man, without all this whispering. I don't like that sort of shushy secret talking in other languages.

Our guide checked his wristwatch and swallowed a sigh. Sir, the priest does not speak English. I serve as translator for you and the priest.

The assistant nodded and smiled at us.

Shoulders stiffened, Sally's husband stood to attention. That doesn't make sense to have a priest who can't speak

English in a tourist church full of Americans. Most of us here now is American. That priest oughta show some respect. Besides, I'm not gonna take off my hat because it's about God and this is a church. My hat says God Bless America. Can you tell the priest what that means? God. Bless. America. I don't want God to stop blessing America just cause I'm inside some French church that supports switchers. Seems to me like we need this flag and its blessing now more than ever.

We pretended to admire the altar, though some of us were not pretending as much as others. I felt the usual chagrin which develops in the company of insensitive chauvinists who travel so they can complain about how a country is different from their homeland.

After a few hurried whispers between the guide and the priest, the guide asked our group's maverick to kindly remove his hat or to wait outside the chapel for the duration of the tour.

Fine by me, he snapped.

Half-turning to his wife, he said more gently, Sally, honey, you feel free to buy you some of those nice praying beads. I'm going to find me some Coke! I've about had my fill of this John and her helpers.

His steps echoed like leftover organ notes. The door creaked shut, its hinges clearly strained.

Our faces lit up when the guide described how the chapel was used for Sunday worship.

Sally said she would do anything to take a tour on Sunday and come to worship.

The tour guide shook his head. Tourists are not allowed in the church on Sunday. Only worshippers are permitted to attend the service.

But I would worship, Sally insisted. All I want is to

worship where Joan worshipped—to be part of that holy moment. I'm not a tourist at all. This is about faith for me.

We knew Sally was a tourist because she'd taken first-row seats on the bus, but we also understood what she meant.

We heard the rustle of linen between legs, a noise from an alcove near the altar. Sally whimpered a litany of dissatisfaction, which sounded religious given her small frame and slightly disheveled bun. Ignoring the guide, she walked slowly toward the front pew in the chapel, the one nearest the altar, and bent her body to kneel. We felt the impact of Sally's bowed head as the guide explained Joan's revelations.

Poor Sally, one of us whispered. First she loses her husband and now This.

We thought *This* might be a reference to the lack of ornate gothic sculpture we had witnessed on other French churches. We thought the word *Poor* described the church as well as Sally. Joan, herself, 'was poor,' we thought. Those of us with lower-income upbringings recalled how being poor lit a match beneath one's buttocks—an urge to grow and get out of the house that wasn't for keeps.

Our thoughts converged on the deity behind the impulse. Joan knelt and asked the Lord what place He had chosen for her. Sally wept and mumbled words without beads. The same G-d heard their prayers.

An unfamiliar rustling noise emerged from behind the alcove—a man whose hair ran down the front of the black linen shirt like a fox pelt.

Who is that? we wondered of the man with the golden red beard that circled his face warily.

We thought him furtive and were relieved to hear the guide announce, Oh, that is the iconographer.

Our eyes widened a bit, hoping he might perform an introduction or at least a liturgical ritual that felt appropriate in such a context. But the guide read his pamphlet and the iconographer's eyes stayed attached to the weeping woman hunched in the pew. Did the iconographer have a problem with Sally? Maybe there was a sign she had missed in French. We had the sense that something untoward was occurring.

What's he doing? one us asked.

He makes icons, said the guide.

He's not making an icon right now, one of us observed.

He is waiting for the paint to dry, I offered.

We seemed relieved by the possibility of a man who had nothing better to do than wait for paint to dry on an icon.

One of us needed to use the restroom. The group divided itself into tufts of grass separated by pavement. Some wanted to look for relics. Others freshened up. There were those who prefered to study the pretty pictures on the wall near the sacristy. Still others discussed Joan's family in hushed voices. I felt an individual need to check on Sally and figure out this strange artist who painted on wood with gold leafing.

Shoes cannot be quiet enough in a chapel. I wondered if the chapel was in fact G-d's womb, and my feet akin to the stomps and rumbles of my son's feet inside my belly. Before others knew or named my sons, I knew them by their kicks, a sign that even in utero a creature would do what he wanted. Even in the chapel, we humans gossiped and argued, passed gas, complained about prices, and intoxicated ourselves with an excess of holy communion.

An icon is a way of thinking about G-d. A thought which concentrates in one human face, an image, a likeness, an unbeautiful object of contemplation. Saint John of Damascus instructed Christ's followers to paint on wood and present for contemplation He who desired to become visible.

I fingered the Joan cards in my pocket and thought about what to say to the iconographer. My images were flimsy cardstock paper and yet they lasted for over twenty years to journey with me to France.

Sally, I said, don't feel bad.

She looked up at me as if she'd swallowed a day-glo lantern and all the light seeped from her face—burnt sienna from the fold of her nostrils, cadmium orange from the hollows of her cheeks, chromium oxide green and ochre from the space around her eyes—a series of halos and oval shapes.

I feel wonderful, Sally sighed.

Icon eyes, whispered the iconographer. He smelled of frankincense and body odor up close. A heavenly father sort of aroma.

Please? I asked in the slow voice I use with the French and other foreigners. *Que?*

I'm American, he said without making American eye contact. I think she has icon eyes. I think this woman has seen something beyond us.

Not aliens, I hoped silently. I couldn't bear to end another day with alien or zombie stories.

The iconographer gazed at Sally in wonder while Sally gazed at the statue of Joan. I was involved in this chain of gazing eyes and this curiousness which stung us all the same time but differently.

She is blessed, he whispered from behind the fox pelt face. She is like a finished icon.

After the paint dries? I prodded.

The iconographer drew his lips downwards into a cringe. No. After paint dries there is nothing but wood and color. The face appears after warm oil is poured over the dried paint and rubbed in. Again the oil and the rubbing. Again and again. Until the image appears and the spirit takes flesh. His voice was solemn and algebraic.

I wondered if the oil dries as well—or if the icon remains oily. Having never touched an icon, I didn't know.

The oil dries, he said in that slow, hallowed lilt.

He reached out and touched Sally's cheek with grubby fingers. At what point do we learn to be careful—to carry or touch things with hands full of care?

See? he held up his hand—dry. The tears on Sally's cheek had evaporated. Maybe there were no tears to begin with. Maybe we had gone about this backwards. The glow was neither oil nor *lacrime*. A holy sheen that didn't leave a face wet. Only wet-looking.

When I was twelve, I tried to paint icons. I made a series of icons about Joan of Arc. Maybe I thought she would protect me. My voice sounded less mature than I remembered being.

The iconographer remained transfixed by Sally. He hardly knew where I was. But we were in this together so I took out the cards and showed them to him.

You made these? he said.

Yes. I made them. When I was twelve. Carried them in my coat pocket everywhere including spend-the-night parties.

The tour guide's voice called us to the back of the chapel. It was time to buy beads and postcards and take our leave of Joan's chapel.

The iconographer ran his fingers across the cards and cocked his head to one side. You made all of these? he asked again.

I nodded. Sally stood up and crossed herself, transfigured by moist-not-wet.

But these are baseball cards! he said worriedly. To put a saint on baseball cards might be blasphemous.

The iconographer stepped back in concern and then crossed himself, eyes following Sally towards the chapel doors. I thanked him for his time, but I don't think he heard me. When I looked again, only the rustle remained.

As we walked out of the chapel, the sunlight assailed us. We covered our eyes with pamphlets. The tour guide stared at something across the street.

Oh look, it's Harold! Sally exclaimed, still radiant from the recent spiritual event. We didn't see a Coke product in his hand.

Hey Harold! Sally waved.

Looks like he's talking to some local man, one of us said.

Harold grinned and waved back. He looked happy. He did not look like the man in the chapel whom we knew as Sally's husband.

The tour guide said it was time to board the bus.

Alrighty, Harold shouted. Let me say goodbye to my friend, here, Pierre—is that right?

A man in black wool pants nodded and shook Harold's hand.

We climbed the metal steps feeling dizzy and depleted as an energized Harold told us he and Pierre had been discussing the best way to cure bacon.

There are traditions to this sort of thing, you know, Harold said buoyantly.

The tour guide instructed us to wave goodbye to Joan's village.

Good-bye, good-bye, little place, Harold chanted.

We said goodbye as well.

On the drive back to the hotel, Harold rubbed Sally's shoulders as she fondled every last one of the Joan cardboard icons. They are marvelous, she gushed.

You could sell these at Little League games and

introduce young Americans to Joan of Arc, Harold added. The entrepreneurship of fellow Americans reassured him about the future of the world. Good things will come of this, he promised.

Please, keep them, I told Harold and Sally.

Yes, I was sure. Their faces plunged towards me like college football fans towards stadium hot dogs. I realized how fragile my insistence on being different from other Joan fans. And then I found myself standing there with Harold and Sally, sure of things together.

TUICA

THERE ARE THOSE OF us who drink *tuica*. There are many types of *tuica* but no *tuica* which is not a traditional Romanian spirit that contains 28-60 percent alcohol by volume prepared only from plums.

There are those of us who never once tasted *tuica*.

There are those of us who cannot drink a beverage which is home-brewed and therefore never once legitimized by an ad.

Regardless of who drinks, there is an appropriate time for *tuica* which descends on the innocent and seasoned alike. I avoid my grandfather's gaze. The tapping motion of knuckles against a small glass. The tap tap tapping he expects to fill his cup and then the clear, water-hue of the *tuica* itself. Add to this the countless *tuica*-gulpers in the park who resemble kind old men getting hydrated.

There are pour-drink gestures which repeat again and again at 11:00 AM. Anywhere in the world at 11:00 AM where one Romanian gathers himself together with the spirits of Romanians past.

It might be easier to understand if *tuica* was a palindrome—but it is not a palindrome.

Easier to understand if *tuica* tasted good—but *tuica* tastes like old sponges dipped in rubbing alcohol, the half of a half-dressed wound. And shit.

The woman sits on a stool and fumbles through recipes. The word tumor pounces from the talk show screen. She should cook liver since it's been a long time and she is the only woman in her knitting circle who knows how to cook liver.

An old man wanders into the den.

The woman becomes a series of skirts and scarves and folk dances. She is a *hora*. She spins like a top outside herself. When she slows, the recipe calls for two large red onions.

Later that night, after the liver and the salad and the heap of napkins scattered like petals across the mahogany table, there is the requisite drinking and joking and poking about. There are corneas painted beneath poise-and-pluck eyebrow armor. There are kisses half-begun in the hallway. There is the scent of a friend's vagina on her husband's breath. And there is the old man on the couch tapping an empty glass.

More *tuica*.

On the porch, her husband flaps his hands and mimics bird calls as a substitute for the emoticon she might have glimpsed of him on screen. She is not allowed to see his emoticons, as a man's emoticons must remain private.

Why? she asks.

The mourning dove is never here at night, he tells her.

There are names which turn into misunderstandings. The constraints of phonetic spelling render more damage than good.

But why does your breath smell like—

Honey, listen. You are wound up like some mechanical toy. It's no good to be wound so tight. I do what I do because therefore I did it. Henceforth, I've done it again.

More *tuica*.

The woman knows that the hurricane on television becomes a tsunami in a matter of time. The victims pile up like slot machine numbers. She knows it is a game but also not a game. People keep dying. There is nothing she can do to stop them.

Nothing.

More *tuica*.

The morning makes its way around a flower pot in small shadow handprints, children singing ring-around-the-rosie, or the silhouette of the song and clasped hands—all the ways light can make much of small things past, all the maggots in the carcass of childhood.

There's no point in thinking the worst. Worse happens whether or not you watch it. At least you can press click and see how to make a green bean casserole. You've never made a green bean casserole. Why don't you make a green bean casserole? I love green bean casseroles made like my mother's with the crunchy canned onions and the Campbell's creamy something. Why don't you make something I like instead of whatever you ate growing up poor?

Hush, she says to the cat who mews for fish-shaped treats. Hush, Oliver—as if you haven't had enough fish to fill a pond already.

I'm all ready for tennis, he tells her on his way past the cat and the casserole and the special cuisenaire. What can I pick up from the Publix on my way home?

Nothing.

More *tuica*.

A teddy bear.

The old man taps his knuckles against the glass.

The husband expresses his enthusiasm for tennis. He is not aware of the old man. He does not remember putting the keys in his ignition when he drives across town. He only knows he needed to arrive and he has done so. The days pass like summer sprawled across a city park.

The woman cooks the casserole she sees on TV. Her husband responds like the screen men with exclamations of delight and satisfaction. Like the men on TV, her husband disappears when the plate has been emptied. Men are accessories for meal time. What use have they apart from eating?

But the old man remains in his chair and waits for *tuica*. He complains that her husband stays out late doing god-knows-what with office women. He uses three toothpicks after every meal.

When the woman sits for a second, the old man places his wrinkled quivering palm over her hand and smiles.

You are my favorite granddaughter, he admits, his love limpid, clockwork, *tuica*.

HUSH HUSH HUSH

THE MOLE ON THE outside of my daughter's left heel is very very dark. It is dark as an ink blot or honest-to-goodness bat-wing black. My mother died two months ago because G-d loved her. Because G-d would spare her the parts of a story where her five-year-old granddaughter fights melanoma. Mole grows darker and larger by the week. I make an appointment with my dermatologist. The voice calling to schedule an appointment is one knot shy of hysteria, one tremble short of losing too much. At the lake, I slather on layers of organic full spectrum sunscreen. I pray over the spectrums that haven't been discovered yet. I pray they stay away from my child's foot. I practice explaining to her why the whole foot must be removed. Why a foot is a piece of shit. Then a lung. Later a liver. My breath comes out in colors I cannot spell. The curses are a call and response I carry along with a universe that might do this to us. Fuck no, I say, knowing the other kids will see what I've hidden *in utero* so long, a little one we called my best nurser, the favorite fail all over my face.

WIND WORDS

for my father

We board The Transylvania in shoes with white soles. Mama argues with Old Professor about air conditioning. She doesn't see why he should run it—there are hatches to leave open, fresh air to draw in. The word *windsock*.

This is not a hotel—the air should be pure. The word *formaldehyde*. The reference to *invisible chemical agents*. My sister and I pretend to comb doll hair.

Old Professor rubs his temples—The air is too damp, it will feel sticky. He wants to sleep.

When Mama speaks, the words snap from her mouth like popcorn—Don't be an Old Man!

The boat moves a little bit like the first part of a pony ride before it gets mechanical. Before the clunk of gears shift. But I *am* an old man, says Old Professor.

Mama pretends to prepare the bed. The word *berth*. She acts like the girl in a sad German story. She doesn't like to read those stories to us at night. She doesn't want us to be sad.

Can we look sad without being sad?

The sad girls wear pretty dresses. It looks pretty when Mama says sad things. The word *sorrow*. The word *regret*.

I tell mama I am thirsty.

She is too busy making the sad bed.

Old Professor offers me a glass of water that is not cold. Maybe it comes from the ocean, which never gets cold.

Thank you, I say really quiet. All the times my voice comes up just a tad shy of a somersault and no one but me is spinning.

The word *marina*. The word *knots*. The way the wind rambles through all the words regardless.

There is night and too-bright day. Mama makes us wear hats and orange puffy jackets. It is hard to play Magic Tower in the jackets so we take them off inside the cabin while mama helps Old Professor. The word *first-mate*. The word *starboard*.

My sister thinks the words must be special types of fish because there is a fishing pole in the cabin. I say no, we are *sailing*. But I wonder if she's right. A starboard sounds yellow.

We see a white feather drifting on the top of the water. The word *seagull*. The feather floats past houses with long wooden decks. Some bird's dress.

Old Professor drops the anchor when the sun turns the water orange. As mama makes dinner, we throw bread to the crooked white birds who pause in the sky like boomerangs.

Seagulls, Old Professor says.

Mama smiles from inside the cabin. When a seagull drops a whitish-gray gel on Old Professor, Mama says it's good luck to be pooped on by a bird. They laugh. The sky is a pink I can't explain with crayons or bubble-gum. The word for this pink is missing.

Inside his palm we see a shiny metal instrument. Old Professor says it is a tool for making music. He plays a song with his mouth moving along the metal.

Mama says he should sing it, so Old Professor folds his hands over the instrument and begins to sing in mama's language. The word is secret. The word is Romanian.

I ask mama what it means.

She watches Old Professor like she's worried—the way she eyes us when we dangle from the magnolia's skinny upper branches. Like she doesn't want anyone to get hurt.

My sister says, Tell us, Mommy.

Old Professor keeps singing as Mama explains: On the night that we two parted, the lake and zephyrs wept…

Mama says he is playing that Romanian song he used to play after too much wine and her mother, Funny Buni, would look away. Can a song burn your eyes if you stare at it?

Mama shrugs and points to the shore—it's a heron. The word is *nesting*.

My sister says, Mommy, I'm cold. Whenever she talks, you can tell she's the baby because she sounds like one. I say *Mama* (not *Mommy*) to make sure we're separate. I am not the baby. The word is *mature*.

Old Professor tries to play the metal again, but there is water coming from his eyes and so he stops. Mama asks him to sing some more. She can't remember the rest of the song. Old Professor clears his throat and sings.

Mama says the words mean humans forget things. She pauses because Old Professor closes his wet eyes. There is a hole in the song he can't get over.

I always thought that was you and Mom's farewell song for Romania—and for your families, Mama says. Before you left.

She wipes her cheek when she thinks we're not watching, but I'm not the baby. The word is *look*.

No, Old Professor says. His voice sounds like it's being blown through a tunnel. His eyes are red with sunset.

It was about your mother, he says. All these times—all these nights—it was about your mother.

Mama says, Shhh. It's okay when the boat rocks. She says, It's okay, we are at anchor.

My sister buries her face in Mama's lap.

I know the anchor can be pulled up on the chain because

Old Professor showed me. Our anchors come back to us.

Mama kisses Old Professor. Says I love you so much, Dad. The next morning, we sail back to the other boats in our orange jackets. The word is *docked*.

We pack two cars and get ready to go back. Mama doesn't want to go. She says Old Professor is lonely. She says lots of things that don't make sense and come out fast. The word is *love*. She says no matter what she does, Old Professor will watch us get smaller and smaller. And distance will be the color we look as we move further away. He will pour a glass of wine and make music from metal and mama will wave. She will wave and wave. And one of them will be what is missing.

THIRTY MINUTES

DANDELIONS SMOTHERED THE FRONT lawn. Never had I witnessed this profusion of asexual, unpollinated blondes engaged in apomixis.

The heat demanded a specific mix of stoicism and languor, a willingness to wilt gently.

Did I lean into the elbow of an Alabama August and wonder what to drink? I don't remember.

Dandelions slumped forward, stems hunched like scoliosis, I discovered myself likewise limp-ish, looking every bit the Poet-Sunk-By-Mrs.

Because Mrs. and missile sound the same when whispered against the paned glass of a kitchen window.

The man came in smelling of sorcery, sycamores, and mid-sidewalk shade. He said howdy then fumed up the room: got vivid with action verbs, sauteed a pan of no-no words, and stomped away the finches at our window feeder.

I told the man he ought not take out shrill workplace matters on my home-struck hide.

I told the man his little rages made it hard for me to draw close and spill my heart about important events, including but not limited to dandelions.

The man gestured televangelist-mad and said he was tired of being blamed for everything. I wasn't exactly a picnic in the park. G-d knows the sink was overflowing with dishes.

See, I sighed, that's what I meant. I can't tell you anything, given what the United States Supreme Court dubbed a chilling effect on speech.

The man's eyes turned sharp and pointy. No telling how

he sharpened them so fast. No telling what the eye-flint equivalent.

He said was tired of being regaled with his faults and shortcomings. How about addressing my faults for a change?

Obviously, I assumed my faults had been addressed in the comment about unwashed dishes. There were many such slights and repetitive sins related to the appearance of the house. Had the man missed the implications nestled within his comments?

The confusion reminded me of the time I protested the playing of She's A Brick House at the progressive dance club. What's so prog about turning a woman into real estate property? I queried the DJ.

It's just a song, the DJ said.

Oh yeah? Well, there are males in the room. At least ten males are dancing. And there is no such thing as a song to males. Haven't you heard what happened to Tupac and Big-E? Don't you keep up with Eminem and Kim?

•

An electric machine made churning noises. The man demanded attention. He expressed hunger and attended my response to the question about faults.

We can talk about my faults, I assured him (dinner being Ramen noodles with shrimp flavor packets). But let's try to address the complaints in chronological order. Let's pretend there's a timeline afoot. Let's start with what I said. First.

The man groaned. Said I was being sneaky. He had to take shit. We could resume this golgi apparatus later.

I said great. I wondered who was sneakier. I was fine with the outcome. A castrating female is not the same thing as an anal plug. Because Mrs. and missive share a consonant with submissive.

•

After a period of prolonged absence which involved a change of clothes, a few YouTube videos, and a ukulele session, the man was ready to resume the discussion.

Given the extent of your electrical-wiring related demands, he said, I have decided to demand something in return.

At the time, we had a neighbor who was a Men's Rights Activist. He left pamphlets in our mailbox listing what men should demand. I tried to remember what the MRA had listed.

I have a demand, the man in the room declared.

An original demand? Or a general one?

It's my demand. An individualistic, localized demand. A native need.

I thought this sounded promising—a firm demand, a little hope, and yes, sex would be grand. Sex was on my pie graph of unmet needs, in the same quadrant as comfort and lovingkindness. Yet the man's eyebrows were not arched in a sex-positive manner.

Every night—at exactly 9:30 PM—we will talk for thirty minutes.

Is that all? I wondered. My heart sank a milliliter.

It will be our priority. At 9:30 PM, the notebooks disappear, the dog is muzzled, the stars die, and we talk for thirty minutes.

Since he referenced the murder of astronomical bodies, I assumed we would not be talking outside on the back porch with cigarettes and wine and maybe reefer.

The man confirmed my suspicion. You get too distracted outside, he said. Owls, etc.

Where will this nightly event be staged? I asked in a multi-lateral tone.

In our bedroom. On the bed.

Once again, I held out hope for complex, innovative foreplay. But when I touched the man's knee, he bristled.

None of that, he snapped. No hanky-panky. We will talk about the relationship.

As if to show me he meant business, the man set an alarm on his wristwatch.

Sure enough, at 9:30 PM, the watch beeped and the man said it was time.

When a watch beeps, can it be anything but time? Isn't a beep how time speaks? I thought about those terrible dandelions, a plant French villagers called *pissenlit* as a result of its strong diuretic effects. *Pissenlit* means pee-in-the-bed. Or so I thought as I carved a space for myself on the bed with the man.

This won't hurt, he promised. You'll get used to it.

The man was being a straight-up, unrepentant cunt-tease with such talk. The man was having fun playing with my head.

Is this playing-with-my-head time? I asked while the man eyed me expectantly from near a plaid linen pillow.

This is time to talk, he said.

About anything?

Of course, he said. Then beamed like a Chevy truck with mondo tires and shiny steel rims.

I checked his forehead for a gun rack.

Why do you take your stress out on me rather than the source of stress itself? I asked. Seems counterproductive.

Oh, he said. I see how this will go. You are going to list my faults and reduce my manhood.

Of course I giggled, seeing as how the man had grown unscientific.

I told him I'm not sure penis size is reducible unless we're talking from the point-of-view of an erection, in which case it's not a reduction in manhood so much as an unsuccessful erection.

He checked his watch.

I waited for him to notice the new Stevie Wonder poster above the dresser. When I looked at Stevie Wonder, all seemed right with the world—but the man looked miserable in comparison. I sealed these thoughts into a tiny secret parcel where it had no fangs. The man would be ruined if he knew what I knew had just happened when I compared him to another man, a man I've only dreamed on a poster.

Close your eyes, I encouraged.

He refused.

You'll never feel like Stevie Wonder with them open. This is what I wanted to say. But didn't. There was a secret and the way small tendrils of hair escaped the ponytail.

The man propped his head on his hand as if he were a nude model extolling sweatpants. He looked nude while fully clothed. I was thinking about his body and how it resembled a not-body despite the expression on his face which was clearly nude.

This is about bad communication patterns, he said.

I was flummoxed. How could he say something so simple in a way that sounded hard to pronounce? The man made ordinary self-help sound French.

I agreed that time would be divided equally for complaints from both communicators.

Time's up, he said. Same time, same place tomorrow.

I'll be sure to dine beforehand, I promised.

And yet—it was the end rhyme of absence, the beat between dine and supine, which stuck in my throat.

•

We met the next night at 9:30 PM on the bed. He

started the timer while reminding me that this would be good for our marriage.

Are we married? I wondered. How did that happen? Surely we didn't...

We discussed the career-related challenges of female stand-up comedians, the terrible shoes worn in work-places, the way whiskey can or can't get rotten, depending. It was rather relaxed.

I feel like this is doing wonders for our relationship, the man remarked. His brow uncurdled, the kink in his jaw, relieved.

But I disagreed.

When I disagreed, I was being disagreeable.

At this point, the man rose from the bed and sought his watch on the dresser. Time was up. He said I didn't have to communicate with him any more if I had better things to do, like maybe fold the laundry or write some dinky stinky haiku.

Can we talk longer than thirty minutes? I asked. Because *dinky* and *stinky* sound better in sonnets. Because form matters when we're limiting syllables.

No, he said. Thirty minutes is enough. Let's not rock the boat. Let's stick to the formula.

I couldn't see how small-talk was a form of worthwhile communication, but the man was a creature of boundaries so I tried to respect them. In a non-literal fashion.

Can we talk about your temper? I asked.

Not if it's one-sided and blame-y.

I don't want to talk about shoes ever again, I admitted.

How about flowers? he offered.

Dandelions?

Those are weeds, he insisted.

Flowering weeds?

Fine, the man said.

I recounted how Mom picked armloads of dandelion leaves and made a salad. If you picked the leaves too late in the season, the salad would taste bitter. A time and a place for everything included a bitter taste. Bitterness was a matter of time for some weeds.

Sounds great, he said. We can talk more about flowering weeds tomorrow night.

The way he said it was as if he had given me an unused prosthetic limb. He said it as if conceding ten feet of soil at Waterloo. As if one thousand eight hundred seconds amounts to magic.

Because *thirty* rhymes with *dirty* and *purty*, I know this thirty-minute story can't have the ending we want. There's no way to inspire confetti in thirty minutes. I feel sorry for the man as well as the person who has gotten this far only to realize it can't go farther.

DANTELLA AT HARVEST

MOM LOOSENS HER ROBE to unstifle the story, red hair flocked like autumn sheep against her face. A Waterhouse painting I won't know until later.

Here is the room with the cheap plastic stars on the ceiling.

Now is the story she hasn't said yet.

•

Once upon a timepiece they don't make anymore, there was a land and villagers who gathered the harvest. In the Carpathians, old women covered their heads with black kerchiefs and propitiated small household icons against rain. All in its time and none too early. Scythes shone gold in the blaze of sunset. Dantella followed her mama into the fields. She watched Mama carry the heavy brown clay jug filled with drinking water. The men were thirsty. She followed Mama through thick belts of mud along the dirt road, careful to tread only inside the footprints left by Mama's boots. The footsteps were far apart for Dantella's tiny legs. As mama strode, Dantella found herself compelled to run, so great was the distance between each step.

•

I know what comes next.

I don't want Dantella to run. Doesn't Dantella pay attention? She shouldn't run.

Mom smiles and rubs the heavy feather comforter.

I sleep beneath thirteen pounds of Transylvanian geese in the state of Alabama. I am a girl who can sleep under anything and still feel wet.

Dantella is doing what she knows to do. Listen to the

story. You can't change a story just because it doesn't suit you, sweetie.

She calls me sweetie often. Her eyes braid blue into my back when I squirm at the symphony. When I daydream through piano lessons. When I lose the receipt from the dress I promised to hold at Pizitz.

Always a sweetie—even when the word slips like smoke from a dragon's throat, even when it coos like hot cocoa from steaming kettle. I am always the sweet thing she stirs in her cauldron of boiling mother love.

•

Dantella ran until the running became all the steps she could take in one lifetime—all the steps ever taken by mothers or sisters or aunts or grandmothers along the rough-hewn road in the field which leads towards the mountain. Away from the village where people knew her name. She ran until the houses became seeds floating on a pond, and the willows were merely old men trundling past.

•

I know it's bad when things trundle past. If there's anything that's evil in this world, I know it comes with forgetting.

No. I don't want her to get lost. I don't want to know what happens to Dantella.

Now now, Mom croons. Life doesn't stop moving just because you press words like red buttons. What's the worst that can happen, sweetie?

Dantella could die.

Mom laughs, the red hair dancing like skirts in a hora. Dantella can't die. She's too curious to die. And besides— *dantella* means *lace* in Romanian. Don't you want to know why? Aren't you wondering how the Romanian word for lace came about?

No. I don't want to know.

Now now, Mom frowns and plucks at loose pillowcase threads. You're not even curious? How is that different from being dead?

The barred owl mourns from the branch outside my bedroom window. He does this each night, even though no owl answers.

Maybe you are the girl who died in the story, Mom whispers as she leans down. But now you'll never know the ending.

Her red hair tickles my cheek, the scent of sesame oil, a kiss upon the forehead.

NOT WITHOUT SOME PAIN

> I've learned, not without some pain,
> to tear the mask from others, but
> my own mask has become my flesh.
> >   —from *Dark Desires and The Others*
> >   by Luisa Valenzuela

> Comrade Professor, are you grading me
> for what I knew then or for what I know
> now?
> >   —Doru Stefanescu

THE HUBCAP COLLECTION

THE TIRE TURNS TOWARDS a cement curb, stops just before impact. The span of seconds between a drip and a tumble of ice from a snow cone. The nick of time.

Suburbs sprawl across former meadows and secret hideouts. Flowering dogwoods, arms which once surrounded us like havens before the future overtook romance we might yet make—if not for landscaping responsibilities. A postcard lies crumpled near the pothole—someone's artifact.

The woman smiles ruefully. It's not her problem.

I watch as she picks it up anyway, and lifts it to her nose, drawing in the scent before flipping it over to read the back. One can only imagine what she reads. One can fall in love with the rest of one's life right here in the unremarkable cul-de-sac.

One can pack up this woman and put her in it.

The postcard is from a son to his mother. He wants his mother to know he is sorry for leaving. But he can't divulge where he is because he doesn't want to come back. The son is only cartoon-sorry. A picture from Calvin and Hobbes, this see-you-later sorry amounts to playground poise.

The once-red Dodge Caravan rumbles past, hubcaps clicking like teeth bumping teeth, and first kiss misses.

I could stand here and tell you stories for hours if it weren't for my hubcap collection. One Hubcap, for the most part, give or take a few I've saved as memories. He's the hub and the rub and the truly-sorry later. He's the stranger part of estrangement, but I'm not keeping score.

For the record. I'm not the scoring type.

•

In the kitchen, Hubcap brews coffee with the French press we received as a wedding present eight years ago.

I wonder if we should plant a garden.

José wants to know why I call him Hubcap.

I say it's because hubcaps make a lot of noise.

He frowns and says there's more to the story.

Just then, Clementine rumbles through the room with her tiny wood car, a percussion of clunks and clatters.

Vrooooooom, vrrrrrooooom, she whoops.

Hubcap pretends to check the expiration date on the Happy Grass-Fed Cows milk carton.

See? Hubcaps are noisy.

As he decants an excess *ker-plunk* of milk into a mug, Hubcap acts as if nothing has changed.

Look, he says, cars make noise, but that doesn't say anything about their components. A human can sing karaoke but not with fingernails. It still takes a voice to carry the tune of what happened.

YOUR SUPERIOR

THERE WAS THE GLASS door to the office you walked past.

There was the smile like a wick you lit without wax when so walking.

There was the glass ceiling you said did not exist and also the fact that I was your boss. Technically, your superior.

There was that night in the pub when I mentioned it. And the pitcher of beer on the table a light yellow, a wan urine hue, a cheap beer you drank with abandon.

There was the way your hand held a beer mug as if to say things were happening—as if to say all over the world things had happened and this could be part of that. A drink could be what happened but also happening.

There was me.

There was a need to remind you that I was your superior. To use that word—*superior*—in all caps and purple font. To make the word sound massive, imposing, and definite. To leave no doubt. More triangle than triage. Not a flexible happening sort of shape.

There was your hand and the nails bit low.

There was an unapproachable hope that you might bite me. Do with me nail-bitten things. There was hope I placed in you and how your hands rose as you spoke double-helix.

There was the scent of Irish Spring soap which could never be childhood again. The soap in my mouth would not wash it. The first taste no longer light or laughable— the wingspan of your palm not a tickle.

There was a sedan parked near the metal trash bins. In the front seat, a streetlamp spilled over my knees and I could tell by the way hands folded she was nervous. I could tell she wanted something from you even if it spilled. Even if it stained.

There was something she wanted like cocaine but softer. Even if she'd never done cocaine and soft was an aperture she never used, a made-up magazine context.

There was desire inside a car bearing its denizens.

There was a vehicle not moving.

There was thunder that could have been the Bruce Springsteen CD.

There was a lull that could have been Nebraska.

There was the kiss that ran down my legs like ice cream seeping out the sides of a cone in a summer you can't stop from dripping.

There was a thing not supposed to happen and what happens anyway after Heidegger—what happens once is a gesture you can't contain in a moment you barely remember.

There was creepage outside the cone of event horizon.

There was never a no.

There was never a maybe.

There was soap and skin and the way steam froths over windows. There was no author of the strokes on the steam that may have been scribbles. There were fingertips—mine and yours—which pressed against the window. Also a smudge which may have been my head. But nothing we could attribute.

There was the office meeting in which you declined to work on my team. I don't know if I like how she manages, you said. Then discomfort as eyes averted.

There was the glissando of your thumb across my lower back as you said it.

There was a skinned knee which stung when my jeans

rubbed against it. A smart and a sting with each step in the office, I felt the repercussions of what we did in the car and how the rain covered us.

There was nothing on your carapace to indicate what happened.

There was no cut or bite-mark or abrasion.

There was the sense in which your palm became a cup I wanted to be poured into. I wanted to say things that forsook grammar for new open spaces which others might read as violations.

There was a paper they would mark red with lines and xxx's.

There was the office meeting when parts stung and smarted, but I felt stupid.

There were those who said you didn't like me; my management style too overbearing and detail-driven.

There was a cigarette break when you rubbed me raw with your too-wet eyes and Irish Spring aroma.

There were workplace rules about managers.

There was my being your superior.

There was pain as the raw knee scabbed and each step I took might crack it open. A rumor you didn't like me. A kiss in the stairwell again and again. A like/unlike aperture. A body inflamed and swollen by inferior events.

There was nothing specific in the workplace manual.

There was a glass ceiling I rammed my head against.

There were windows in a car and cups of me spilled over.

There was being diminished and yet acting bigger.

There was why and why and why but not in earnest.

There was no earnest why.

There was come over.

There was how much I wanted and what you knew better.

There was rattle and hum as buses flew past and you

told me I was not your superior. You would never permit a female above you.

There was the matelassae of your lips on my neck and the murmurmurmuring of what you wanted being equal. Two pairs of eyes, over-riveted. Two bodies broken into gears. Two forms of time and all of us present.

There was a thing I knew about time from road trips.

There was a thing I knew about desire from how a knee burns stiff.

There was someone you imagined and someone you avoided. There was the Foucault you'd never read.

There was a time when we were equals.

There is this. There is Now. A page on which I pressure you. An ink by which I am always yours. A story which renders one superior.

BUT WHO LOOKS
GOOD IN LATEX?

THE STROBE LIGHT ADDS static to the canvas. It blurs the image, divides one portion from another. I'm starting to think strobe anything bodes bad for integrity.

There are the thoughts trampling through my head as I gulp cheap porto and devise compliments for the unremarkable midwestern pastel landscapes. When Kaitlin waltzes over to ask for impressions, I say it feels extraordinary—like a lightning storm on the prairie. I say I'm impressed by her implied critique of modernity, given that mechanical strobes are all we know of lightning on the plains.

Oh I love you *soooo* much, Kaitlin coos, linking her arm through mine. I knew you would get it. Now if you can just wander round and enlighten the critics.

The room flashes and vibrates under the impact of wanton electricity and furtive voices. A waft of White Diamonds perfume leads me to wonder if I am in the middle of psychaedelic electrocardiogram. The pressure to make small-talk is intense.

How long did you spend in the field to paint these? I ask Kaitlin.

She gawks. Silly, I have never set foot outside of New York state. Mostly I borrowed from Thomas Hart or back issues of *National Geographic.*

At a loss for authentic words, I tell her they look like the real deal.

But I've never seen the prairie either and so I am stuck

with this feeling that the critique is not right. The 1980's drug sensation mingles with the realization that Kaitlin cannot disparage all the viewers who will only see fake lightning on prairies and mistake it for witness, since she's never seen the prairie and there is no one here in an authentic position to say anything whatsoever about lightning.

No one is authentic anymore, I venture. Look at my husband.

We glance towards the food display, where Hubcap, who is my husband, my *eine kleine* something, veers back and forth between jalapeno poppers and blueberry cheesecake. From the way he stacks his plastic plate, you'd never know he's two days shy of a colonoscopy. The anesthesia causes amnesia—he can't remember anything except waking up near an old man singing German bar songs. Hospital recovery rooms are replete with old men singing German bar songs. It could be any hospital in the world.

Question of origin: So how did you come up with the idea for this series?

Kaitlin smiles and waves at a group of females bobbing around the door, but no one sees her. She smiles and waves again. This is her night.

Well, she sighs cheerily, it sort of just came to me all at once while I was waiting for this guy I met on Match.com to come out of the bar restroom. He was from Iowa and I couldn't think of much to talk about, and then the strobe lights jiggled my brain a little and I decided to maybe ask about lightning in Iowa. Or prairie fires. Remember how my little brother loved to try and start prairie fires in the backyard when we were home for summer in the week before camp started—but it never worked out? It's not as if there were prairies in Mississippi.

I remember her little brother. How is Harry doing anyway?

Harry is doing everything possible to revive cultural norms which prohibit the viewing of female ankles. He's having a blast.

Harry, a prude? I can't see it.

After all, Harry's penis was the first male organ to whom I was personally introduced. His name was Hank. I never told Kaitlin about my adventures with Hank on a campground in east Tennessee. From Hank to Harry—wasn't that a Neil Young song?

Kaitlin toys with her jade impact-necklace—But anyway, so, the idea came like a bolt from the blue. Originally I'd planned a series of portraits in various love-lit locations. Portraits of a woman over time, a female fabricating the future of her marriage and assuming some things wouldn't change. I planned for her to lose an arm first and then a leg and then an eye, but I wasn't sure viewers would get it. The purpose, I mean.

Oh? I was one of the viewers who struggled with metadata in gallery spaces. I'd taken classes to help uncover the meaning of life, but colors muddled the picture. I could do the meaning of life in black and white but if I added a little gray or yellow, I was a goner. And Kaitlin is still talking about the *punctum*.

You know—how she keeps losing things she didn't plan to lose so she becomes a totally different sort of creature while her idea of marriage remains the same. But the lightning reaches out to more people, I think. The potential for impact is bigger. Like Venedikt Erofeev versus Turgenev—more modern and localized. Just look at all that prairie.

Kaitlin waves her arm around the room giddily. At which

point, I notice Hubcap once again attacking the final three peppers.

Kaitlin, you should mingle. I'm going to fill the critics' ears with praises. Kiss kiss.

He feigns surprised when I walk over to the table and say in my casual Lana Turner impression, Howdy-doodie, Hubcap.

Oh heyyyy, honey, I'm teetering a bit over here. But your breasts would look fantastic on a xerox machine right about now. I could make front and back copies.

Downshifting into late Judy Garland, I tell him: I think we should go. I think you should give me the keys. I think you could have looked really good in latex later tonight if you weren't so plastered.

You must be referring to some lay-text, he slurs before vomiting a glorious assemblage of organic materials which resembles a fair-trade Afghan quilt on the gallery floor.

Bye-bye, I sing and wave to no one who waves back. My goal has gone from art appreciation to vomit-scene avoidance in less than one minute.

Hubcap continues to vomit various colors on the drive home and then vomits green pepper skins for three hours at full throttle.

I climb into bed angry and dissatisfied after having indulged fantasies of light bondage involving my grandmother's paisley silk scarf, for a greater part of the evening. The fantasies must have been provoked by the pastels.

As I fall asleep, I overhear Hubcap reciting Bruce Springsteen lyrics to Trotsky, our mini-poodle.

I'd sing if I could, but every time I try, it's like a *vomitus maximus* trigger. Sorry Trotsky.

He feels bad for not belting out Bruce to the canine. He feels like the canine has been deprived of something.

I don't want to think about deprivation, but it's the last thought on my screen before the pixels dissolve into sleep.

When I wake up, morning creeps through the windows with a sunless aroma. I'm not the in mood for rain today. Maybe I could lay here and pretend nothing is happening.

Instead, there is the kitchen, where Hubcap wants to share my coffee and it's too much too fast. Too much to assume things will pick up from the part of last night that he remembers. It's typical Hubcap. He smells like fennel toothpaste and I have no unused words for how lonely it feels to wake up on a Saturday morning conscious that he was too drunk to have sex.

He tries to kiss me.

The kids are watching cartoons.

Come on, Sugarthighs, let's give this coffee a run for its money.

No. I push him away.

Not now, I say. Later.

The word is a cathedral bell clanging and clanging. His face is not going to church.

When you say we'll do it later, I know you're not telling the truth, but I don't know which truth you're not telling, he says.

I don't know either. Since when do I owe this man one version of a story? The house feels like high school jeans—tight around the hip and knee joints—and I can't move. Maybe I'm paralyzed. I say I'm going to look for an umbrella. He follows me out the door into the garage that smells like wet cardboard. We are stuck inside the resonant moisture of old boxed things on a day when we should be hiking. On a morning after we should have had sex.

Hubcap peers around. It's time to throw some shit out, he says. The time has come to leave some shit on the roadside curb and then watch from the kitchen window to see who wants it. Who wants what.

Who knows?

This is leftover data from a marketing class he took in college a year after we first slept together. Since then, not a single billboard is innocent. Even *Jesus Saves* wants something. What's the difference between that and Goethe? Selling your soul to the devil or to G-d is a cash exchange either way. No grace is freely given.

The stacked stuff hurts my head. I don't want to do what it wants me to do and then feel briefly magazine-fresh. I never feel like I'm supposed to feel after doing what I'm supposed to do to feel good about myself.

I realize I should have slept with that physics major at the gas station while Hubcap was still sleeping with his ex.

What are you thinking? he asks.

I don't know, I say. Honest. Because I'm done thinking about the physics major.

I don't know which part of here-now-home will be true tomorrow. People lose limbs everyday. I never know which thing is a lie until I tell it. Then after I've told it, I stare at the part that sounds wrong. Maybe I'm lying.

Is it normal to not know what you're thinking? Hubcap asks. I mean, I guess it's slightly Marxist to be an alienated bourgeois, but is it normal to feel that way?

I shrug and stare at the boxes. Hubcap keeps probing and prodding. In honor of feeling however normal, I'd like to observe a moment of silence with you, honey.

We stand quietly, but the train blazes its horn through Hubcap's silence.

I glance up, this time not trying to avoid his eyes. It feels like a dare given how the dark grows bright between us. I want the immunity offered by the blue glow from a late-night television screen, but the silence is too busy. There is too much to say and so much we want from each other. He wants my coffee; I want a magic coat woven from his curly black chest hair. He wants to love me; I want to be loved in a less time-consuming manner. He wants to give away the pets; I want to bury them in the backyard like I read in that story. But nobody's talking. We are standing in the garage in the center of a get-busy, bustling silence—and the soundlessness of what should be said is a split lip, all puffy, busted-open, large print.

AND I NEVER
UNDERSTOOD CALCULUS
OR THEORETICAL
NUMBER GAMES

He said your head hurts.

She said how do you know?

He said your face is drawn and the color is gray but also blotchy.

She said it is almost time to go.

He said what about your head and are you sure?

She said we could die tomorrow and what would it matter.

He said it must be a migraine.

She said we could die today on the drive to the theatre anything can happen, even if it's not what you planned. Even without a ticket.

He said we've been planning this for a long time and I hate to waste the tickets.

She said you can put them on the fridge under the Humane Society magnet.

He said why do you hate animals?

She said I don't know.

He said why.

She said what do you.

He said if you hate animals.

She said I can barely see your eyes that's how bad it hurts.

He said people are animals too.

She said the pain is like whatchoomacallit behind my right eye and is my head still attached to my torso?

He said you try to avoid things.

She said where.

He said here we are, going nowhere and not the theatre and now we're doing it again.

She said hurt me.

He said I can't.

He said there's too much competition.

He said what about the baby feral cats run over by cars and have you thought about that?

DISNEY ONCE, DISNEY TWICE, DISNEY...

THE RAIN SMOTHERS THE dog-toothed violets near the old pine stump. I witness their hopeless struggle to stay aright. A storm this strong snaps the neck of every red tulip. Sometimes there is nothing you can do except watch and be sorry.

Only one tulip is broken, Hubcap clarifies. The other fifteen look absolutely fine.

Remind me never to call you as a witness if something important happens in my life.

He cocks his head, towhee-like. Now don't be like that, he pleads.

Oh. Oh I wouldn't dream of it. I'm going to be like this instead—a little morose, edging on maudlin, aware of how climate change impacts the flowers, and not a word he says will budge me from feeling sorry about it. Not a single word will lift me from sadness and sudden regret.

Because he hasn't even read Yevgeny Zamyatin (not to mention Czeslaw Milosz) so he wouldn't know a velvet prison if he wore it to church. He doesn't know what can happen. What always does.

Nothing happened, honey. The plants got watered. A few earthworms threw a party. Things got festive and wet. Meanwhile, our rain barrel was replenished.

And that's how it looks from here. To Hubcap, what you see is the entire story.

I can feel the frayed edge of his off-season shorts brush

across my mid-autumn thigh. We are both inappropriate but prone to different seasonal misappropriations—his the beer swills of early summer, mine the vivid brutality of early fall.

Erosion? He shakes his head, baffled and bemused.

The Latin word *rodere* means to grow or to chew. I can see the soil being chewed away and returned as mud.

Hubcap sighs and wipes his palm across his shorts.

Sometimes I don't recognize you, he murmurs. There are times when I don't know who you are.

His problem—not mine—for I know what I am is a sum of remembered presents, a collection of past-tense verbs pursued into all possible futures.

To know what you are is not the same as knowing who you are.

So be it: the fact that sound travels eleven hundred feet per second does not explain why we cannot hear each other across a small room. The desire to draw closer is stymied by an aversion to what is foreign—to what lies outside the believable-ness of bodies. It's no mystery why anxiety-riddled males prefer sealed, impenetrable national borders, but marriage is a porous institution, a vehicle that absorbs more than it bounds.

The green tank top falls off one shoulder, but I am not a fixer—my self-consciousness does not extend to the realm of corrective action, only to the awareness itself.

To the knowledge that it has fallen.

This happened. It rained. The flowers died. My tank fell off my shoulder.

I sense the twine of a sentence he starts and the blank space after it. The unfinished business. The chilling effect of honest sadness on domestic free speech. Sad is where I'm standing. I am bubble-wrap thick with sadness until

Hubcap mentions our summer vacation. Until he says in no particular tone, We should do something different this year.

Like Sudan? Fascinating history there—the kids would learn so much.

Actually, no. Not Sudan. I need a new passport.

From the way he crosses and uncrosses his legs, I can tell something is bothering him. But mentioning it will bother him even more because there will be double the bother-somes—a bother-sum—one which he doesn't want to say, and the other that his wife just articulated. A sum of bothers will ensue.

You wouldn't bob about like that if you didn't already have a plan of sorts, I tell him.

Well—yes. Since you mentioned it. How about Disneyworld?

The cough gives me a moment to compose the WTF.

And what the WTF makes you think I'd find that appealing?

Also the expletive—Disneyworld—sealed with a scowl.

Well, my parents offered to pay—

Come on my what?

He blushes. They want their grandchildren to have a memorable vacation.

A memoraWTF?

Well, an American vacation. There's a lot of history stuff there. Epcot Center. Constitutions.

American? Americanismo? You mean, as in, the history of the place? Its essence?

It would mean a lot to them, honey.

But we swore never to take our kids there. We swore never to celebrate mindless consumerism. I can't believe you're seriously saying this. It would mean a lot to them to shove something we oppose down our throats? And then take pictures? To demonstrate once and for all the prowess of manipulation?

Hubcap looks sad—Maybe it's their version of spinach—but also slightly angry.

Spinach is healthy. That's why parents force it. Is he arguing for the health benefits of Disneyworldland?

It's not a big deal! His eyes grow squinty. Why do you have to make it such a big deal?

Remember how crazy I went when my stepmother suggested the same thing two years ago? Because my parents never did that to us. They never took us to a place where consumption was the only object.

What about Six Flags?

My sadness has evaporated into meteor-raging madness. Why are we having this conversation? I want to kick him in the shin or step on his toe—something that hurts and snaps him back to his senses. But my credo of nonviolence restricts our physical communication. Mad and mad and madder.

Look, Hubcap—how about being honest for a change? Why don't you tell a true story and let's hit up Coney Island because that's the real America. That's the sordid, fascinating show where freaks and horrors are commodified, and we pay to see the stuff our parents warn us about. Hairy palm shit.

It's the part I appreciate—the dark, seamy side of capitalism, how it trains us to approach difference as spectators. Cash in hand. Something we pay to see. I love Coney Island. I want to be buried on Coney Island.

Hairy palm shit?

I nod. There are not enough vowels in the English language to describe Coney Island.

Well, I guess. He bites a thumbnail and looks up warily. I've never actually visited Coney Island…

Seriously?? I don't believe it.

My parents thought it wasn't good for us—too freaky and strange. You know, the focus on abnormal people and stuff.

But I don't know.

I don't know what it means to be normal when it excludes half the world who can't afford it. I don't know what it means to have fun that looks like fake plastic trees and princess jargon. Disney is dangerous. But Coney Island—no one on Coney is hiding anything. Coney Island is safe. Openly freakish. There are hundreds of purple, green, and orange mermaids on Coney—there is a rainbow of mermaiding rather than just brand Ariel.

I want to show him how Coney Island is a sister to Ellis Island—smeared with the fingerprints of untranslated emotions—tired, weary, yearning, eager to breathe free. Coney and Ellis speak to the immigrant in me. But there are moments when honesty appears as a bluff, a strategy to hide a losing hand. At this moment, I aim for the facts, and not the sentiments which Hubcap has little reason to believe.

I say: Coney Island is more American than Bud Light and silicon implants, which are relative newcomers to the homeland scene if you think about it.

I say: Don't Disney me and leave punctuation open.

THE ROMANIAN PART

for Carla

I CAN'T SLEEP. EACH tick is a tock wherein consciousness recreates the world. What we see becomes the thing we can't see past. The face of a stranger seen twice is something else: the face of a familiar stranger. A table is anything you do with it—locus for Thanksgiving meals, a homework habitat, a depository for vases and collections, a fond, quick fuck set—the vision reveals our intent.

Insomniacs know this. An insomniac knows the way her mind interacts with an object is a story about her mind. What I think about the nightgown says more about my mind, more than the white cotton material at hand.

How the world can end in a nuclear accident.

How we use an old hankie.

How we encounter a porch screen.

The minivan's inner cluck.

What we make of a thing is the story of us.

A story I can't sleep with. An ending I can't sleep without.

If I weren't dying of every symptom I google, I might find time to save this story. To make something commendable of what looks like a mess from the door-frame. But time is running out and my death could be hours away—a big-rig truck bearing chicken thighs from Kansas, the world's fastest cancer, a splinter infected by staph. The possible ways I might die reduce the possibility of sleep. Sleep will never be possible given what I know about the likelihood of strokes.

Clear as Sunday comics, I will never sleep again.

Clear as Superbowl cleavage, I will die of never sleeping and someone will drop by to say they told me so.

The owl outside the window hoots three times. Then it hoots again—a single, lonely hoot.

I surmise Hubcap has been reading things when he leans over my pillow and says in his somber, very serious voice: *No matter what happens, I am never going to leave you.*

The lilt's open arms indicate he wants confirmation. The silence confirms he waits for a response. Time ticks and ticks and ticks.

Should I say, *That's right honey*, maybe look demure and salvationish as I permit the white tank nightgown to slip off a summer-bronzed shoulder while gazing into his sad Eeyore eyes?

Is that your mother's nightgown? he queries.

Of course. I'm wearing Mom all around town. And whatever's left.

He's trying his Tiger Badge bestest, but Mom laid the terrestrial foundations for how it feels to be loved and no one can ever love me enough again. Enough is a strong meter. A husband's love is affordable given the firmament of mom's underlying love. Given that first love laid down as a premise. A brick in the street. What some might call a roadblock. If only it felt firm, roadblock-like.

Which it doesn't. What's left without her scowling, scolding, hard-rock love is a squishy, sloppy mud pit. What's left is a girl in a too-big night-gown learning how love is a house blown down. Don't tell me there's a fucking mystery here. Mud is one slippery way to drown. Mud is the sink that drags me down into the dark, primitive vernacular of my Romanian parts.

This is where I begin. This is what Hubcap married. This

is the story that wanders back. Nine years ago. Once upon a shindig.

The Romanian Party

I feel better about my Romanian parts after Hubcap survives the first party. Not only survives but opens his eyes wide as a fawn and kisses me because—Hey, that was something else.

You could still call off the wedding, I say. The invitations haven't gone out.

Are you kidding? Why would I do that? I had a great time.

I try to believe him, but something in me fails to connect the Romanian girl with her American variant.

This was the garage party. The one where middle-aged adults joined the elderly on a dance floor improvised from a car garage complete with karaoke and disco ball. The one where Mrs. Zamifirescu sang Loretta Lynn on repeat. There is nothing as heartbreaking as a Romanian accent dipped in southern twang after four shots of home-brewed plum brandy, there is nothing like standing by your man when you are spun.

If Hubcap looks happy, it's because this is his dominant emotion.

What he doesn't realize is that many things happen that night without really happening. Because they happen in a foreign language.

Because they happen in words he can't understand, these things didn't happen to him. Sometimes I can't believe how many things don't happen to Americans standing in the same room as what happens.

Here's what happened to everyone except the American guests. Ana brought a newly-divorced friend to the party;

Ana attracts new friends like cockleburs on the back of a sock.

This is my friend Tanya, Ana beamed, and she's not from Romania, but I wanted to show her we Romanians are full of hospitality.

Ana didn't have to tell us where Tanya was from. There were welcome remarks and rapid-fire signs of the cross.

Acting as if the Communist Occupation never took place, Mrs. Tudorescu cozied up to Tanya and revealed the Romanian community's open secret, specifically, the best place in town to find cow tongue was Piggly Wiggly.

White Americans only know how to cook with two animal parts, she sighed. But the black ones still use hooves and stomach and guts. Yes, Piggly Wiggly has good meat and a real butcher. I pledge allegiance to the Piggly-Wiggly.

Tanya giggled and wiggled. Recently abandoned by an American husband who worked for Coca-Cola, she was doing her best to fit in. She met her husband by mail and what bloomed was a classic epistolary romance.

We fells in the love at first letter, she admitted lispfully, golden curls bouncing off the walls of a heavily-fortified cleavage.

Her voice drooped to a little girl whimper—But after I come here to him I leaves my parent in the Russia, this husband no love me anymore. He say I not as nice as ze letter.

A wisp of innocence in her voice toyed with bravado, endowing the saga with unexpected complexity, a sense of multiple molecular layers. Tanya might have been a heroine in a novel by Dostoevsky if it weren't for the neon magenta lipstick and the black go-go boots.

I nodded in sympathy (her story confirmed what I'd long thought about the rottenness of the Coca-Cola corporate entity) as I sought the appropriate dancing rhythm for the karaoke version of 9 to 5. Leave it to Tanya to make like a missile towards the dance floor, where she invented rhythms I'd never imagined, carried along by the momentum of two massive breasts clapping like hands until you felt good about yourself. Despite your self. Until you thought, They must be clapping for me.

Really, it was the usual party.

Followed by the consequent car ride.

The Consequent Car Ride

Did you see what happened to the old widower Dumitrescu?

Hubcap shakes his head as he rubs his palms over the steering wheel. He barely remembers the names. Seriously. It was all -escus to him.

Well, I hope Ana learned a lesson, at least. It's never a good idea to bring a Russian to a Romanian party. PTSD—and stuff.

Who was the Russian? Hubcap asks, conveying genuine interest as he mans the turn signal with skill.

Oh *come on*. Don't tell me you didn't know who stuck out from the crowd—with her headlights blaring like a World War II tank straight through the gentle streets of downtown Bucharest! Don't tell me you didn't notice who was bent on conquest.

He chuckles. That blond lady? Tanya?

The Russian, I confirm. The Russian who hooked up with...

—the old man who had a wooden cane?

Hubcap covers his mouth, but laughter escapes like Easter eggs from a toddler's basket. I *love* Romanians, he confesses.

She was NOT Romanian, I emphasize hoarsely. Russians are not Romanians.

I swear it's like the Roosevelt-Stalin Pact on repeat.

Hubcap doesn't have to know any history. He knows the US Constitution is a work of art, and liberals who like to bring up slavery or Native Americans are just trying to steal money from hardworking American taxpayers.

As for getting married, he wouldn't miss that party for the world. He idles the engine and puts his palm over my hand. He calls me honey. He says: I love your reaction to things, honey. I love how you get around them. How you get around the Romanian part.

The Romanian part. It's like a lazy eye one can't avoid noticing; nevertheless, there's no reason to mention it. It doesn't come up often. Usually in public first-sight situations where the difference demands explanation. But also on holidays or when skinny dipping or at religious moments. Like the apocalypse. But mostly, it's not mentioned.

Her Best Romanian Child

And so we wed. We marry and marry in white under-awning.

After the wedding, Hubcap expresses unrivaled interest in forthcoming Romanian parties. He develops a taste for *sarmale* and *ciorba*. He jots down recipes for *tuica*. His shirts carry the sharp scent of cabbage into our bed.

I am stuck in my Romanian head—startled out of it when Mom says he is her best Romanian child. It doesn't seem fair to award the title to someone who escaped the most humiliating years of garlic perfume. I remind Mom he's not Romanian by blood.

Hubcap hides behind stove pot steam. When he emerges from the vapors, his face looks flatter than any cake I've ever baked. His feelings are wounded.

Why do you have to draw lines like that? he asks. Life

is not a nation-state. Love is not a thing that permits geographic borders.

I tell him he doesn't understand. Life is not a melting pot. Love is not a bag of purple jelly beans. Literally. What happens in Romanian stays Romanian.

And yes—things will get bloody.

Please observe the left eye on the stove where someone is boiling a tongue.

The Hello Kitty Journal of A Catholic Schoolgirl Who Isn't Catholic

When he finds me reading Hello Kitty diaries from my Catholic schoolgirl days, he asks what I'm trying to find.

I tell him the truth: my childhood.

What have you found?

Cabbage. Cartloads of stewing cabbage. A clear lack of personal space. A conspicuous absence of privacy. A language which has no word for teenager and no expression approximating 'terrible twos.' My mother's gentle hands, everywhere.

Sounds like you had a strong family identity.

A strong family identity and my parents' American dream. Two reckless Romanians who defected from Ceauşescu's Communist paradise and worked like animals until they made enough money to wear their upper income brackets to church. A sailboat. They outdid themselves, my parents. They outdid themselves all the way through that fabulous, all-American divorce.

The honey spills out. I know it was hard for you, honey.

Hubcap's sympathy is half-shade and baseball cap boyhood.

You don't know. It was very hard. It was like the breakup of Yugoslavia.

Was there a Tito equivalent? He's channeling *The Big Lebowski*.

Romania was Tito. Tito was the Romanian part. Even if he was not Romanian. He acted like one, holding things together.

At least they both remarried Americans…. he exclaims.

At least your face hasn't been punched yet.

Only an American husband could be such a callous optimist while running his mouth over scar tissue.

The Kitchen Saudade

When he smiles, his eyes transform into tiny jubilant earthworms, unseasonably merry wriggles. Hubcap's happiness electrocutes me from my well-tended stupor.

What are you doing? he asks.

Remembering things. Trying to find the Romanian part.

He smiles again, those reckless little earthworms. Have you looked in the mirror? That nose is a start.

No, that's the Roman part. I'm looking for what's Romanian. Since Mom's death, I've grown more desperate in my pursuits of history.

Hubcap grows pensive, strokes his unshaven chin. We need to change the oil in your car, he finally admits.

He's a good man, but I don't have time to notice. Maybe I should be a better wife. A fun, Amy Poehlerish wife. A female who stays funny even after divorce.

Are we getting a divorce? Have we discussed it?

He stands with one hand in his pocket, shaking his head, wanting to know (and know and know and know) what I'm thinking.

Amy Poehler. She's funny.

I don't want to worry him.

First effort: I sing, Baby, you can drive my car…. to the oil change place.

For a second, we laugh, belt out the remaining lyrics together. But I can feel the tears warming—the expiration hour on how long can we enjoy being stupid—the weight of What Isn't mounting behind the eyes.

Honey, he begs, What is it this time?

As if time is a chronology of crying events centered around the Romanian part.

Lacrime, I say, weepishly.

It's the Romanian word for tears. A Latin word he knows through experience.

My little *lacrimosa* he whispers affectionately, drawing me into the fold between his armpit and his sweater where the aroma of sweat meets natural, patchouli-heavy laundry detergent. I think back to that Phish show when my cats got out of the tent and I found them before an old capital-ist hippie sold them to Phish-heads from Ontario. Things could be worse.

I have an idea! Let's make your mother happy.

And *whoosh*—Hubcap is happy again. It doesn't take much.

Mom is dead, I remind him between sobs.

Exactly! What—you don't think she can be happy with-out all this material stuff around her? You don't think she can enjoy an eternity of eavesdropping, and watching the people she loves most without being interrupted by work or dinner or DayTimers?

I don't think she can…—it's hard to say aloud.

…see us. Hubcap fills in the blank.

I nod, slurping up the snot meandering across my chin.

Wellllll, maybe that's just it. Maybe you've gotten too caught up in the American part. Maybe you don't *believe* in the Romanian part anymore. We don't have to go all

Kierkegaard on life, honey. There's room for either and or in this universe.

For some reason, a phrase slips out. In the stillness of time, I mutter, trying to recollect when I heard it, followed by relief when Hubcap ignores me and begins to rummage through kitchen cabinets, stacking clear Mason Jars and drinking glasses on the black countertop. Then he opens the fridge and removes the entire vegetable drawer before piling an obscene harvest of grocery store discounts—cucumbers, green cabbage, garlic, carrots, green tomatoes, celery—near the glistening choir of glass jars. Now, he declares with gusto, let's get started!

With what? I gulp. Because I have a sordid history with kitchen activities.

Muraturii. And making your mother happy.

For those in the dark, *muraturii*, translated picklings, are a brine-soaked potage of any conceivable unripe vegetable left to pickle, or mur-mutate, in jars with salt and spice. Any decent Romanian has a recipe handed down through generations so the act of making *muraturii* swells into a seance complete with arguments from disgruntled mothers-in-law, sighs from weary uncles. The ghosts of any Romanian family rise from the grave and congregate around the table to participate in the ritual.

I hear Mom telling Hubcap to boil the water twice. She thinks he takes too many short-cuts. I hear my grandfather Claude saying Mom doesn't know anything—a female physician has no place in the kitchen of his youth. I see Dad sipping his Merlot and playing the harmonica alongside the percussion of restless pots and pans.

Yes, I tell Hubcap. We should make *muraturii*. We are in good company.

As Mom pours the brine back and forth between large

metal vessels, my grandmother, Turica, proceeds to empty the cemetery plats of Sibiu one by one, recounting each member by name. Who had enough horses, who married for a carriage. I see the shelves of her Bucharest pantry burgeoning with bottles of marinated vegetables. What became of the cabbage boiled and sealed in jars, enclosed like family nicknames, inside jokes, local legends—did she feed the old ghosts to visitors, or did she reserve her pickles for second comings? When she died alone in her art-infused apartment, did she pass her *muraturii* along to next of kin? Hubcap is curious. He didn't expect company.

When I attempt to translate the story, my throat clots up again. Choke and try not to cry at that sustained level, which turns into full-on, fainting-couch style sobbing.

What am I thinking?

I am thinking that, here, we would throw my dead grandmother's *muraturii* to the curb. You can't make money off pickles at an estate sale, my American part chides. Our family values are monetized. Spirit doesn't sell.

Despite his insistent interest in my thoughts, Hubcap pretends not to hear me. He's busy hanging with the Romanians right now. I shiver. Soften. Join him.

I watch Mom hold up a jar of *muraturii* against weak window light, the cauliflowers swirling like debutantes, a cotillion of cauliflowers dancing wistfully. She puckers her lips, eyes checking the skin behind cauliflower ears for specks of dirt or grime, before pressing her mouth against the glass and giving the jar a smoochy, PG-13 kiss. Perfect, she whispers, these particular dolorous dithyrambs familiar. Familiar and familial.

My Romanian Parts

I try to bring up our exes. It seems lighter than blood, and less dangerous.

Tell me about your college girlfriend, I beg. Give me the bang-bang of American-on-American. Shock me with perved-out details.

Instead, Hubcap describes dismal misunderstandings and an angst richer than a Save the Whales sticker campaign.

I admire his capacity for commercial melancholia. Then I smile. Then I frown. Then I feel terrible as a violin breaks my heart in the background, a string quartet for college girlfriends, fellow humans, people who have hurt and been hurt, the walking, everyday wounded.

What is envy? I wonder. What could there be to envy about a fellow human being if being human means feeling impossible, splendid, broken-into-bitties—and aren't we all feeling it?

Hubcap says maybe some feel more than others. Like me, for example, feeling excluded.

An unavoidable inert alien-nation, I rebuff. Totally post-Marxist. Blame it on Wilsonian idealism and the rise of the nation-state.

When he leaves the room in search of wailing child, I don't think about college or girlfriends or threesomes. Instead, I return to the noisy, intimate, Romanian part—a public without privacy tucked inside a heart , which can't decipher tailgating parties. Romanians don't sustain high levels of festive excitement and drunkenness for anything short of a funeral or revolution.

I am a corpus divided, a body half-decked with phantom limbs and two languages in which half my body parts don't acknowledge the other. The part that aches is never present.

I feel smothered and abandoned. At the same time. I say this to Hubcap as he brushes Banjo's hair. And then later when he feeds our useless mini poodle, the same thing— Smothered. Abandoned. Maybe overwhelmed.

He says I should borrow a page from Rilke. Not the page about abandoning one's spouse and child in order to live alone and be a solitary writer. That page was lame, he says. What Hubcap appreciates is the page from Rilke's letters about how humans are stuck between terror and avoidance. When faced with the uncertainties of life—or the mysterious eternity of death—we can't help but ogle the horror.

You like horror movies, I accuse. For no good reason.

I like what Rilke finds behind horror. *Something familiar and intimate, and of such intensity that my feelings fail me in describing whether it is burning hot or icy cold.*

Maybe it's both? I hope.

Either and or, he says.

Do you really believe that?

He laughs. Why shouldn't he? He's known what he wanted from life since we met. Hubcap is clear and limpid as an active cowbell. Truth is, I'm what's rusted. I am the ill-fitting, hollow part. I'm the part that makes the wrong sounds.

No honey, he sighs. As if I just pooped on the teal-checkered carpet. You're the poet. You're the part that has to say what no else wants to feel. You have to say it and feel it for us.

His fingertips brush my cheek carefully, like a mother palpating fallen apples for the bruises hidden beneath soft, mushy flesh.

I'm not a poet, I manage.

But his hands unite in an active conspiracy against my melancholy. Oh but you are…

You can't tell me who I am….

And you are…

Am not.

And you are and you are and you are—you are what I want, Irina. You are what I want and then some….

Oh Lord, I'm thinking, here comes the weird sex request I've read about in his mother's pro-marriage magazines. My cheeks feel like rubber chickens between his palms. The man is a fiend for eye contact.

I want the parts that don't fit, I want the shit on our shoes…. Irina, I want the Romanian part.

What can I tell you that isn't maudlin literary fiction? Truth is a lie we weave from radish roots. This is one of those times when a sex scene would be nice but I didn't get pregnant until later.

Tell the truth, he warns. Don't chicken out.

We had sex. I can't sleep.

When we stand naked, side-by-side, before the bedroom mirror, Hubcap says it's not about sex. Even though it's obviously what happened. But not to him. Love is what he likes to credit. What love does to flesh, Hubcap says, *that's* the Romanian part.

EXTENDED FAMILY IS AN EMAIL WITH ALL CAPS

I DON'T KNOW ABOUT extended family emails that seem harmless at first huff. One breath and the head balloons. Before the headache splits a skull which is separate. Whose aspirin is personal.

I don't know about extended family emails with accompanying media. See attachment, a photo from a beach resort in Bali with an advertisement for forty-three years of marriage underneath what resembles a belt. All the sand is white, and the waves wander between turquoise and teal. Oh that's such a nice beach. How luxe. What a celebration. You two must be over the moon with happy-go-lucky. You look so relaxed, even though there isn't a person in the photo attachment, really you look more relaxed than ever. The platitude is a native species we're exporting everywhere Mastercard is accepted. The platitude is one big button we press to send.

I don't know about extended family emails but Bali sounds great. Our waiter at the Japanese restaurant was from Bali. He's been working here eight years to send money back to his wife and three sons. It takes eight months of money to buy a ticket to visit his family. He can't afford to waste eight months. But he is happy to serve us today.

I don't know about extended family emails when Hubcap tells the waiter his parents are in Bali. The waiter tries to sing Happy Birthday but a massive salmon-pink resort clogs his throat. Oh the beaches are beautiful in Bali. This must be a song from somewhere else.

I don't know about extended family emails in which my in-laws advertise the benefits of long-term marriage. Looks nice but my mind goes back to the Duggars and how they've been married for so many years and photos where Michelle smiles, her lips a seam stitched across time. The stitch is pretty but not as pretty as some muzzles I've seen in Los Angeles with tiny pink rhinestones. I don't know what years mean except silver and gold. The postcard is pretty but what are we celebrating except maybe a procession of steps taken through time at which point we blow confetti and birth new platitudes.

The thing about platitudes is that new ones look like old ones so you can't tell which couple's anniversary birthed which platitude. In profile they all look the same.

What I don't know about extended family emails is how Duggars stick together on the same screens where dryer sheets promise to reduce static cling. Static sounds like stasis, which is a lie we tell each other about electrons. A lie is not a platitude. A Duggar should not be the celebration of a marriage that fails to end.

I don't know about extended family emails clinging like a choir of voices, clanging like a tower of bells. I don't know about the chorus of birds in the park. I don't know what comprises a song no one intended to sing. The tune is marital triumphalism but the lyrics look like an argument about kitchen paint, ochre or goldenrod. Once upon a time there was a flower but now we have extended family emails. A can of soda left open tastes flat by late afternoon.

HUBCAP, FROG,
AND LUNA MOTH

THE BULLFROG SOUNDS LIKE an insect amid the clutter of a mid-summer Alabama night.

Hubcap disagrees. He insists it is a clear though unattractive mating call. To Hubcap's credit, he has memory issues inherited from the weaker maternal gene pool. And he'd be the first to admit he rarely remembers our conversations, which is why he keeps a notebook in his pocket at all times. This selective memory notebook doesn't include last week's conversation about the bullfrog call. Nor does it include the Google search and National Audubon Society field recordings we used to discern this call is not a make-love-with-me call but a hey-what's-up call.

Hubcap says it's all the same.

I say he's projecting.

Hubcap says testosterone endows his voice with this projectile-like boom. To Hubcap's credit, he has memory issues loosely related to early coursework in American heritage, which is not the same thing as American history, but tonight Hubcap is stuck on the heavy chords of the bullfrog's horniness and the flesh that fits a bull's horns.

Tonight Hubcap's logorrhea resembles inner city graffiti, a thing one sees after mainlining crack under the bridge. Too good for everyday life.

I don't understand why he bothers to get angry and excited all at once. Or why he believes that someone with a rotten memory has the right to exhibit indignant pre-copulatory behavior. I guess it's a bull thing. Ev-psychers would urge me to plaster my genes elsewhere but when I point this out, he says ev-psych is bunch of baloney funded by Big Pharm to winnow its way into the Human Genome Project. It's the most interesting thing he's said all night. But he won't remember saying it tomorrow.

•

In the morning, Hubcap makes coffee with the French press we received as a wedding present eight years ago. I wonder if French presses get rusty. Hubcap wants to know why I call him Hubcap.

I say it's because hubcaps make a lot of noise.

He says that isn't true. Am I grumpy about losing the chronology of pyramids argument last night? Hubcaps are decorative and silent. They make their owners look good.

I assure him that hubcaps are, in fact, noisy.

After stacking three enamel mugs on the shelf, Hubcap says: I think I know why you call me Hubcap. Because it sounds like husband. Or hubby, for short.

We already talked about this. I just explained why I call you Hubcap. Didn't that happen?

Yes, but I don't agree.

You can't not agree with that being my reason. You can say the reason strikes you as silly or inauthentic, but you can't tell me why I do things—like why I call you Hubcap. Because it's my reason.

Hubcap snickers and feigns a counter-swoon.

Here we go again, he says. Am I being sexist?

I nod because it's obvious.

Fine, he says. Can you acknowledge there might be a shred of truth to what I'm saying?

If I do that, you will use it as an excuse to be sexist in

the future. And that would be bad for our marriage. And for you. As a person.

What if I say it's bad for me when you don't acknowledge that I'm at least a teensy bit right?

Then I won't believe you.

•

We wandered into the backyard to drink coffee and discuss what on earth to do with ourselves on this childfree Saturday morning. Hubcap considered mowing the lawn but decided next week was probably better.

If you have ever watched a luna moth spend a day drying its brilliant neon wings on a wood fence, then you might understands the challenges Hubcap and I face in our marriage. Should-I-say-or-should-I-go challenges. Beauty-vs.-agony challenges. Is-waiting-pointless-and-silly challenges. Did-you-see-that-too challenges.

The luna moth resembled a large folk art bead when it caught Hubcap's eye on the red brick side of our house at 9:47 A.M. A tiny pea-green leaf unfurled from the bead's back. And then another. The bead was not a bead. It was beautiful. It was 9:54. We couldn't believe what we were seeing.

This is a luna moth drying its wings, said Hubcap in the voice he reserves for the first two minutes after drinking red wine from the communion chalice.

Our mouths widened into those tiny *o*'s once common in British novels about childhood. Since no one reads British novels about childhood anymore, our mouths widened into those tiny *o*'s found on YouTube videos under titles like soft porn surprise. Only after I observe Hubcap's expression of soft porn wonder do I question the authenticity of my own. His parted lips are clearly closer to those of a hot dog commercial than any awe I've seen.

Do you suppose modern technology has anything to do with that silly look on your face? I ask.

Of course not! It's the miracle of life.

Hubcap's voice remains calm, but the truth is that most miracles, the ones we've had the pleasure to witness, are manufactured for our consumption (like the Space Race), and Hubcap and I, like most good Americans, consume whatever comes our way with an installment plan attached. Hubcap favors installment plans for their secondary effects. Hubcap says installment plans invoke a sense of gratitude once a month when we are reminded of the massive red riding lawnmower he rarely uses, and maybe we should light a red candle of thanks but we don't. Not for the lawnmower. A moment of silence while we try to sort out where the money will come from but that's the extent of our praise-be yippee.

Do you think gratitude is something we should learn by purchasing things we can't afford?

The question wanders away without answer because Hubcap is riveted. The luna moth's wings are now open and trembling. The slightest breeze shakes them like a tsunami. I realize the luna moth is a delicate quivering mass of wet wings on a brick wall, and the parallels to Hamlet alarm me.

Did you see that? Hubcap exclaims. It is 10:18 and the luna moth is inching across the wall.

The luna moth is inching across the wall! Hubcap exclaims at 10:31 shortly before the paper-thin wings lift to launch the moth upwards and onto the wooden fence a few feet away.

Holy shit! Hubcap exclaims before dashing into the house, presumably to retrieve a photographic device of decent, installment-plan character. The luna moth opens its wings from the place it has found on the fence. I watch it and try to imagine what it is thinking. Then I feel guilty for anthropomorphizing the moth.

•

It is 10:41 when I begin whispering jibberish and baby talk to the moth—speaking to it as a subject rather than an object.

It is 10:43 when I realize the moth is not a subject, and I am guilty of anthropomorphizing again, albeit in a more subtle, therapist-style manner.

It is 10:46 when I realize Hubcap has not returned from his indoor errand. I watch the luna moth without wondering what it is thinking and without attempting to communicate. This lasts for one minute before I feel overwhelmed by the pressure of all the words I am holding inside.

Hubcap returns, gleeful minus camera.

I inquire about what is missing.

Hubcap laughs and tries to hug me. He says it wasn't what I thought because I always read him wrong. He sounds encyclopedic as he reports having delivered an important and sizable bowel movement. An accumulation of one day's tabouli and corn cobs. A miracle of life.

•

The luna moth has two circles on its wings. These circles resemble holograms. Hubcap searches for hidden meaning. He attempts to access the underside of universal code. I feel he is using the moth for his own purposes. I feel he is treating the moth as an object.

It is 11:07, and the end rhyme is not enough. Hubcap makes a reference to Beckett. We talk about the guy I dated briefly who referenced Beckett whenever there was a line at the gas station pump. Hubcap asks numerous yes or no questions and then asks why we are, once again, talking about my ex-boyfriends.

It's a rhetorical question because he wasn't technically my boyfriend.

How do you define boyfriend? asks Hubcap.

A boyfriend is someone you sleep with more than once, and it is 11:12. The luna moth has two long tendrils dangling from the bottom of its body. They are wavy, like tendrils. They are absolutely tendril-like. Hubcap says Soundgarden's Fresh Tendrils is one of the darkest songs he knows. The sun is hot. It burns our eyes. Hubcap tries to sing the lyrics. I wonder what the luna moth is thinking.

Hubcap says we are privileged to witness this momentous event.

I don't want to be privileged. My white privilege makes me feel sick and miserable.

Imagine how it feels to be me, exclaims Hubcap. I suffer from white privilege and male privilege! Possibly even Southern Baptist privilege, which is similar to Catholic privilege but more text-based and judgmental.

I don't envy Hubcap's privilege. My favorite writers wrote their best work in prison cells. I think going to prison would be good for me.

Unless you got executed, Hubcap adds.

It's true that execution would not be good for me. It's true that this me is a fragile thing. Though not as fragile as yonder luna moth.

Hubcap says I don't have to die to become a better person.

It is 11:35, and we are drinking a growler of Druid City Brewery's saison. Hubcap says we need a hammock.

But we have a hammock. It's in the garage.

Hubcap says we need a place to hang the hammock. Also the thingies with which to hang a hammock. We need the hammock to be hung. Hubcap says to limit Christ's suffering to the afternoon of the crucifixion is a form of blasphemy. He says there are three versions of Judas.

I didn't know you like Borges.

He doesn't like most things, really, but that doesn't mean he hasn't been influenced by them.

I say maybe the luna moth has three versions as well.

That's not where he was going but Hubcap is a benevolent soul and therefore willing to grant metamorphosis given the miracle of life. Though he wishes the miracle of life included hammocks.

•

I need to know if he's a nihilist. It's a question we avoid after watching *The Big Lebowski* because we want to watch it again, and a serious post-viewing conversation might spoil future things. We want the movies we love to stay funny. If I mention nihilism now, I'll ruin the hours we've spent watching the luna moth dry its wings. The whole effort we've exerted together will be tainted.

I wish this could go on forever, Hubcap sighs.

It is two minutes until noon. Half-time music from a very important game drifts through the yard. Gets tangled in honeysuckle and comes out sweet with sinew. Though the luna moth is mute, I know he is wondering about how it would feel to live forever. On the other hand, he may be relieved that brevity is associated with clarity. He may be a Hemingway fan. He may be glad life's meaning is certain—reproduce and die.

If we lived forever—me, Hubcap, and the luna moth— we might be forced to invent creation myths. Everything we did might be taken as a moral lesson, a parable, the fodder for holy writ.

Hubcap says he would never want to be a god. One day is fine by him. Add one more day for frivolity, and you have all the life you need. He doesn't want to be in prison the way people put G-d in prison. Hubcap needs to know this whole show will end. He needs to know there is an expiration date. The longing for hammocks flummoxed by the laziness, which prevents him from actively pursuing his dreams.

A hammock is a dream, and it is 12:29. We are famished, but the moth could finish drying any minute, and we don't want to miss it. We would feel cruddy if we missed the miracle of life.

Hubcap asks if I remember that Borges story about the cool-but-not-flirty girl named Emma Zunz. The one where the death of Emma father is the only thing that happened in the world, and it will go one happening endlessly. *In perpetuum.*

The fact that I don't remember is arousing. The fact that Hubcap does remember is arousing. The fact that he might be inventing the story and yet managing to convey Borges' sense of time is the last straw.

You are some hot shit, I say, and we begin to make out on the un-mowed lawn. When we finish making out, it is 1:07. The luna moth is gone.

I try not to cry because we missed it. We didn't get to watch the split second when the moth flew away in search of its death. The whole thing is like a mix of Poe and post-*Duino* Rilke, and it's hard to hold back the tears given the combination of pulp novels, craven nightingales, and dying.

Hubcap's cheeks are flushed, and the back of his neck is sweaty. He smiles at me with un-flossed teeth. But my heart is breaking, and my clavicle hurts, and the unbelievable effort of things seems rather pointless.

Come on, baby, Hubcap says, it's just the way things roll, given the miracle of life. The miracle of life is the only thing that ever happened in this world, and it goes on happening endlessly.

When he kisses me, his lips taste of salt and craft beer. This miracle of life is a salted stupor—that we can kiss until the cows come home even though we don't have cows or bison, even though the luna moth is gone, probably hidden behind privet bushes having sex for the first and last time of its life. The first and last time forever is as miracle as it gets.

VOTIVE FOR A MOTIVE

O tell me the meaning. This angel or clod?
I find on her body no witness of God.
—Mihai Eminescu

My sad face speaks across the unswept hardwood, a cul-mination of clumsy parenting forgeries and bad bedside manners, bullet points I haven't learned about how to be a good wife, how to wifey myself and come out wiser.

Damn solves nothing. This salty tongue couldn't nav-igate the ocean if we got waylaid on a random islet. My curses are careless gestures, which demonstrate a failure to model proper coping mechanisms in front of the children. They will plant bombs in gas stations and join lame terror-ist organizations with other overly-entitled brats. An*d Shit* is all I've got in the toolkit?

I like you just the way you are, he declares just before requesting that I change into pants befitting a mature female of my status and stature.

Before asking me to change into a wife, he considers sad-ness—what it is, how it tastes. He discerns something sad about grown women dressing like teenagers. He mourns the nobility and unassuming modesty of clamdiggers and polo shirts.

Against the foreground of a stable family life, I find a background of insecurity. It is my pissy face that steps up to bat.

What's wrong with jeggings?

Oh honey, I love your jeggings. At home. In the yard. At

an 80's costume party. But why not slip into black slacks and an elegant sweater? I'd hate for my co-workers to get the wrong impression.

It is my riot-girl face that tells him the wrong impression is precisely what I hope to effect. All other impressions are fuckable. My cheap Manic Panic lavender hair could not care less about their fancy cupcake frost-jobs. My slutty pants will be an improvement over whatever wife-box they're cramming us into.

You use this *They* term broadly, he warns.

Then: Don't be such a sucker for bad attention.

It is my first-love face that says some like it hot.

It is my seventh-love face that says I'm not going to some washed-out event where people dinoflagellate the room, smiling like barracudas who aren't actually flesh-eating fish because it's not the right metaphor. Rather, it's not the metaphor Bruce Springsteen alludes to in Brilliant Disguise (which makes José's list of top 100 songs). And I'm not going to play by their rules or anything. I'm just going to say har har. Patch over eye. *Enfant terrible.*

Is this about the bikini wax?

It is my WOW avatar face that says you don't know who I am. Because I am not some pop country song fraught with plurals and fancy boots. I am not a shitty tune you can't help humming in the car or while folding laundry. I am not a generic sentiment stuck like bubble-gum to a shoe that is your head.

Look. baby, I've never liked bikini waxes.

Also: I'm not attracted to prepubescent girls. It feels wrong to see you standing there with just a sliver of *pubus*—

The technical term is *landing strip.*

—With a landing strip given that I am not an airplane. Even if I was an airplane, I wouldn't want to land. Though possibly I might enjoy parking? But an airplane can't do the verbs I like most since what I'd prefer is to camp out for the weekend and convey my appreciation for native wildlife.

It is my freshly-waxed face that says you have a talent for making me look unattractive to myself. No. It's a habit. Stop it.

Honey, the magic forest will grow back.

It is my reckless Girl Scout face that wants him to hold me in the hidden space behind the door and tell me it isn't a big deal about the cookies. The grannies will be glad I ate them because they were trying to be solicitous and neighborly and no one eats Thin Mints. Except me.

José pauses. There is something going, and jeggings may look like the iceberg, but it's only the lettuce tip. Am I right, honey?

Lick me hold me love me kiss me anything anything anything. Except it is my wifey face that can't assemble an answer. It is my marital face that floats around the room wondering what is a hive, and can I help, and what are we doing?

It's not the face he wants.

He's not talking to wifey.

So it is the Joan of Arc on horseback face that admits the world changed when she turned nineteen. A perfect portion of the world stolen, and she'd never found a picture to replace the original Bob Ross. When Jim showed her the porn, those perfect moments of masturbatory bliss were replaced by the dullest, most clinical choreography, and Jim grinned and sprang an erection, and Joan said, Damn you Jim for ruining my fantasy life with your rubber-face floozies. I want to go back to the perfect freedom I knew as a child when it was only me, my hand, maybe the stuffed lamb with large beady eyes, and anything in the world could *still* happen. Especially behind the pink velour sofa in the basement, anything could happen, see? Then Jim showed his video, and there's just this or that.

You didn't like it, José surmises.

I didn't like being forced out of one face and into those other faces. The willing-and-eager-to-service faces. The Service Merchandise faces. It is only honest face that says I will not be a wifey. This honest face matches my secret face, which thinks porn-face is too wifey, and porn might be the best argument against marriage, all those faces riveted by penis.

José tries to touch my face. I can feel the soreness where a pimple will soon sprout. What face do you want?

I want to be the face that I was the first time I came. The anything-can-happen face. The first-come-never-serve face. The face blushing when you watch me climb out of the shower for the 742nd time.

What are you?

All the others. The baby steps and the leaps over canyon. How we got here. Vows packed up quick, luggage trundled, words shaken and jumbled in the back of honeymoon cars. When we open the trunk, we recognize our letters but can't read them. Roads turn words into other words. All the right bones in place but not making a skeleton.

A line leaps forward birthing baby lines, promises of first times for everything we have and we hold—a crippled cardinal, a basket of fresh purple tomatoes, a little girl with skinned knees in our arms another promise enlarges a space for each other now an arena into which others intrude. This is why I can't remember the things you swore on that November night when words were wings (and I, in white) exoskeletal pinpricks flesh by fast. I can't remember the others your eyes swore off. Our eyes met like swords jangling together. A match is a round but also a flame's first step.

I love you through crickets and banjos, and the first frost no one saw coming.

I love you so much I ignored everything you said. Years later, I wonder what I'm doing in a king bed as your lips exhale the final bow of a dream. I wonder what have we done with all these words that liberate us from loving another without freeing us from longing. The first step away from a line is longing to go back. Together. Know our way into wretchedness, the inflexible emotion, a ferris wheel car. And a barn must have a ladder into its upper stacks.

HE TAKES HIS
WAKING SLOW

Hubcap is too distraught for coffee. He can't find his keys. The dry cleaner kept the white shirt he planned to wear today. Oh, and you wouldn't believe the nightmare he had last night—the nightmare that kept on going even after he woke up and went back to sleep. The double-rounded nightmare.

•

I say tell me about it.

•

He pauses. Looks up from under a hedgerow of mussed hair with wild eyes. A coyote in the bushes. He doesn't know if he should tell. It was seriously dreadful. He still can't believe it. I pretend to sketch a vase on the thin white skin inside my arm. This is a diversion tactic to keep Hubcap from feeling like he has to share. But the tactic doesn't work because Hubcap starts pacing. He thinks if he describes the nightmare, exposes it to daylight, it will lose its hold over his mind. He hopes to be unhaunted.

•

Gila monsters? I try to keep it casual.

•

If only. No. Much crazier. It was about you. Your skin turned gray, and your cheeks were all sunken in like moon craters. You were a zombie—an eerie, wraithlike, miserable zombie! But also still yourself. Still witty. Still standoffish. Honestly, those traits suited you more as a zombie than in your human version. Maybe zombies seem dead or lifeless in movies but you didn't seem dead so much as jaded. A pure jadedness.

•

He is not trying to hurt my feelings, and yet it hurts to hear myself described as ideal in zombie form. As if the human part of me is missing an essential brick, maybe a basic human brick. I don't want to parse this so I ask what happened next.

•

Well, you were there like an urn of unspilled ashes—creepy but, nonetheless, my wife. *You were my wife!* It wasn't your fault you'd become a zombie, and things looked gray. I wanted to run and save myself because a human and a zombie can't coexist—one has to destroy the other—and to *destroy* is just two letters switched around from *de-story*—and I didn't want to destroy or de-story you, but I didn't want to be destroyed either. Running seemed like the wise thing to do.

•

I agree. I would have run. Maybe posted a warning on Facebook while pausing to catch my breath behind a woodpile but run like a good kite wind. Did you run?

•

Well, I woke up horrified—you were laying beside me in bed, snorkling—which made me feel better so I went back to sleep only to find the nightmare began again. Picked up where it left off at that junction of critical decision—to run from my zombie wife or to stand there in shock.

•

I tell him the suspense is too much. I tell him he might have another nightmare on his hands if he doesn't finish the story. A nightmare isn't a story, but both can be cliffhangers, and that's where I am right now, hanging off the cliff of what next.

•

He grins, dumbstruck, happy as the last hole on a mini-golf course, one of those expressions I can't explain or understand. Another mystery of life—how the things that make him happy are often the things that make me sad about the world.

•

You started to grab my hand and then looked at me—made eye contact—and then placed my middle finger into your mouth and started chewing. I could hear the tiny bones breaking, and it sounded like cereal crunch. You were eating my fingers, and I was watching because I let you do it, see? I let you eat me alive because I didn't want to be apart from you. I didn't just sit there paralyzed by fear, honey. I *chose* to be consumed.

•

I tell him that's the sickest thing I've ever heard. Seriously.

The sickest.

And yet it isn't entirely sick because it sounds true—not true in the real-life sense but true in the existential sense. True as in choosing to die so something you value more than your own life might live on.

I tell Hubcap it's the most romantic thing I've ever heard, and maybe existential problems can only be explained through particle physics and zombie hypotheticals. Maybe zombie dreams are all we have left to say true things: *I love you, I'm here, You're killing me.*

ACKNOWLEDGMENTS

I am deeply grateful to the editors and staff of the journals in which these pieces were first published, including:

82 Review: Doppelganger
Broad! Magazine: Me and Birdie
Cease, Cows: P.C.B.
Change Seven: Wind Words
Corium Magazine: Your Superior
Duende: Tuica
Fiction Southeast: Mother-In-Law Collection
Full of Crow: Cabin Pressure
Ginosko Literary Journal: Mothers Who Die
Minola Review: Toketwat
NANO Fiction: Hush Hush Hush
New Delta Review: White Tennis Shoes
Noble Gas Quarterly: Something About Sunshine in Scrapyards and Woman Rendered Speechless By Sunset
Parcel: Hubcap, Frog, and Luna Moth
PoemMemoirStory: Carpool
Potluck Magazine: Extended Family Is An Email With All Caps
Rivet Journal: Owls
Sandy River Review: My Name Is Not Rita
Shadowgraph Quarterly: A Sport We Use to Pass the Time
Split Lit Magazine: Dear Committee for the Socialization of Illegal Immigrants
The Gravity of the Thing: Our Friend Mia
The Journal of Compressed Creative Arts: Two Faces

The Zodiac Review: Rental Units
Tinge Magazine: 7 Stories About Girl Scars

EPIGRAPHS

Slits for Eyes: Vladimir Nabokov, *Bend Sinister* (Penguin Modern Classics, 2001)

Where I Place My Finger: Luisa Valenzuela, *Dark Desires and The Others* (Dalkey Archive)

From Nothing to One: Leonard Cohen, lyrics from "You Know Who I Am"

There Was No More Blood Than A Period: Title for this section taken from Kathy Acker *Empire of the Senseless* (Grove Press, 1988). Epigraph from Flann O'Brien, *The Third Policeman*

Not Without Some Pain: Luisa Valenzuela, *Dark Desires and The Others* (Dalkey Archive); Quotation credited to my father in conversation about a personal event during Ceaușescu's dictatorship of Romania.

The title for the story "He Takes His Waking Slow" was adapted from "The Waking," a beautiful poem by Theodore Roethke.

Deep gratitude to Brent Spencer and Jonis Agee for selecting this strange little manuscript as the winner of the Brighthorse Prize. There is no way to describe how their generosity and insight has illuminated my world. Extra special thanks to the following journals and editors who encouraged me to continue writing fiction: Lauren Becker for nominating "Your Superior" for 2016 *Best Small Fictions*; *Glimmer Train* for naming "The Chance of That Happening" a finalist in their 2016 Very Short Fiction Story Contest; Ander Monson for judging the 2015

Ryan Gibbs Flash Fiction contest and for seeing something special in "White Tennis Shoes"; Tracey Guzman for naming "Hubcap, Frog, and Luna Moth" a finalist in the 2015 Helen Short Story Prize; Andrew and Emma, for featuring me and working with me and being a source of great inspiration and encouragement; Amanda Miska and Kaitlyn Andrews-Rice for warming my hands and keeping the Split Lit fire raging Randall Brown, for expanding my conception of compressed prose; Robin Richardson, for accepting a difficult piece and inspiring confidence in my surlier stories; Laura Theobald for being Laura Theobald; Amy Burns for accepting one of the first and therefore urging me onwards; Georgia Bellas for reading me aloud to strangers, and my children, and the moon—how to thank the moon enough? How to thank a world missing my beautiful mother?

ABOUT THE AUTHOR

Alina Stefanescu was born in Romania and raised in Alabama, where she currently resides with her partner and three outspoken young mammals. Her poetry and prose have been published in *Cloudbank, Duende, New South, VOLT*, as well as other journals. Her debut fiction collection, *Every Mask I Tried On*, won the 2016 Brighthorse Prize. Her first poetry collection, *Stories to Read Aloud To Your Fetus*, is forthcoming from Finishing Line Press. A multiple Pushcart nominee, Alina is currently working on her first novel as well as a poetry and fiction collection. Learn more online at www.alinastefanescu.com.

CPSIA information can be obtained
at www.ICGtesting.com
Printed in the USA
BVOW11s0705110518
515761BV00001B/18/P